THE
EDUCATION
OF A
DAUGHTER

THE
EDUCATION
OF A
DAUGHTER

BY
ARCHBISHOP FENELON

APPLEWOOD BOOKS
BEDFORD, MASSACHUSETTS

The Education of a Daughter was first published in America in 1847 by John Murphy & Co. of Baltimore.

Applewood Books would like to thank the Fort Scott National Historic Site, Fort Scott, Kansas, for their help in reprinting this book.

ISBN 1-55709-427-6

Thank you for purchasing an Applewood Book. Applewood reprints America's lively classics — books from the past that are still of interest to modern readers. For a free copy of our current catalog, please write to: Applewood Books, P.O. Box 365, Bedford, MA 01730.

10 9 8 7 6 5 4 3 2

Library of Congress Catalog Card Number: 95-78660

CONTENTS.

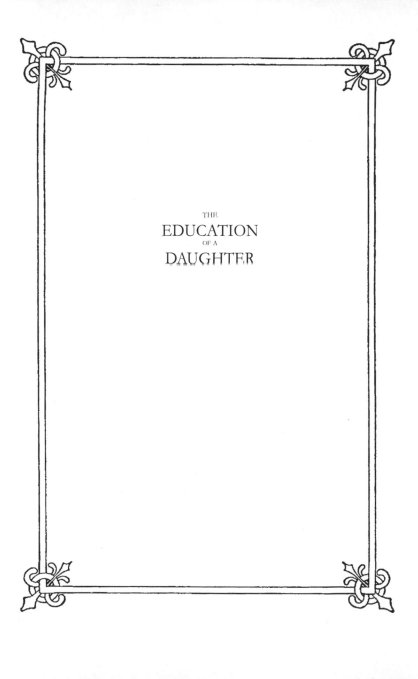

THE
EDUCATION
OF A
DAUGHTER

THE

EDUCATION OF DAUGHTERS.

CHAPTER I.

ON THE IMPORTANCE OF THE EDUCATION
OF DAUGHTERS.

OTHING is more neglected than the education of girls. The custom and caprice of mothers often decide the subject; and generally it is thought unnecessary to give females much instruction. The education of boys is considered important to the public good, and though no fewer faults are committed with respect to the latter than to the former, yet we persuade ourselves that it is necessary to gain greater lights on what regards the education of boys, than on that which relates to girls, in order to succeed in it. The most skilful men have applied themselves to give rules on the subject. How many masters and colleges do we not see erect-

ed for this purpose? What expenses in the publication of books, in scientific researches, in methods of learning languages, and in the choice of professors? All these great preparations have often more of appearance than solidity; but they mark the high idea we have of the education of boys. As for girls, it is said that it is not necessary that they should be learned; that curiosity makes them vain and conceited; that it is sufficient if they know how to govern their families, and obey their husbands without reasoning. The example of many women whom knowledge has rendered ridiculous, is for ever quoted; after which, it is thought right to abandon girls blindly to the conduct of ignorant and indiscreet mothers. It is true, there must be caution not to make females ridiculous, by making them over-learned. Women have generally minds more weak, and more inquisitive than men. It is not proper to engage them in studies which take them out of their proper sphere of action. It is not the business of women either to govern the state, to carry on war, or to enter into the holy ministry; they may therefore dispense with certain extended points of knowledge which concern polity, the military art, jurisprudence, philosophy, and theology. Generally speaking, the greater part of mechanical arts are not suited to them. They are formed for moderate exercises; their bodies, as well as their minds, are weaker than those of men. Nature has

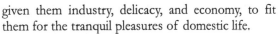

given them industry, delicacy, and economy, to fit them for the tranquil pleasures of domestic life.

But what ought we to infer from the natural weakness of women? The weaker they are, the more important it is to strengthen them. Have they not duties to fulfil, which are the foundations of all human life? Is it not women who attend to and support the whole domestic economy of our houses, and who decide upon what most nearly concerns mankind?—Hence they are the principal source of the good or the bad morals of society at large. A judicious woman, who is diligent and religious, is the soul of the family. She regulates its temporal and spiritual good. Men, who have even authority in public, cannot by their deliberation establish any effectual good, if they be not aided by women in the execution of it.

The world is not a phantom; it is an assemblage of families; and who can regulate these families with a care more exact than women, who by their natural authority, and assiduity in their houses, possess the advantage of being more careful and attentive, more industrious, insinuating, and persuasive? Can men hope to gain any happiness in life, if their closest connection, which is that of marriage, should be turned to bitterness? What will become of children, who will in the end form the human race, if their mothers spoil them in their early years? Behold, then, the occupations of women, which are not less

important to the public than those of men; since they have a house to regulate, a husband to render happy, and children to educate well: add also, that virtue is of no less importance to women than to men — without speaking of the good or evil they may cause to society — are they not half of the human race, redeemed with the blood of Jesus Christ, and destined to eternal life?

We must also consider the good which women may produce when they are well educated, and the evil which they cause to the world when they have not such an education as inspires them with virtue. It is certain that the bad education of women produces more evil than that of men, since the disorderly conduct of men often arises, either from the bad education they receive from their mothers, or from the passions with which they are inspired by other women, in a more advanced age.

What intrigues does history present us with, what overturning of laws, and of morals; what bloody wars, what innovations in religion, what revolutions in the state caused by the mis-conduct of women! Behold a proof of the importance of a good education of females; let us seek the means of obtaining it.

CHAPTER II.

INCONVENIENCE OF THE COMMON MODE
OF EDUCATION.

THE ignorance of a girl is the cause of the weariness which she suffers, as she knows not how to occupy herself innocently. When she arrives at a certain age, without having applied herself to any solid occupation, she can acquire neither a taste nor relish for it. Whatever is serious, appears to her dull;—whatever requires continued attention, fatigues her: the propensity to pleasure, so strong in youth; the example of persons of the same age, who are plunged in amusements, all contribute to make her dread a life of regularity and industry. In her early years she wants experience and authority, to superintend the house of her parents. She knows not even the importance of applying herself to it, unless her mother have taken pains to point it out to her. Should she be of high birth, she is exempt from the necessity of manual occupation; she will therefore only apply herself to accidental pursuits,

because she is told that it is fashionable for women to work, and this will often be an appearance only of employment, not a custom of regular occupation.

In this state, what will she do? The company of a mother, who observes her, who chides her, who believes that to bring up her child well, she must pardon nothing; who assumes an air of austerity, who makes her feel her ill humor, and who appears always oppressed by domestic cares, thwarts and discourages her. She has around her flattering women, who seek to insinuate themselves into her favor, by low and dangerous compliances with all her fancies, who converse with her on all that can disgust her with good. Piety appears to her a tiresome occupation, and her regular rule the enemy of all pleasures. How then must she occupy herself? In nothing useful.

This inapplication becomes at length an incurable habit.

Here is then a great void, which we cannot hope to fill up by any thing solid; frivolity must take its place. In this state of inactivity, a girl gives herself up to idleness, which is the vacancy of the soul and an inexhaustible source of weariness. She accustoms herself to sleep one-third more than is necessary for the preservation of health. This long sleep serves only to weaken, and to render her more delicate, more exposed to bodily infirmities, whereas a moderate degree of sleep, accompanied with regular

exercise, renders a person gay, vigorous, and robust; which makes the true perfection of the body, without speaking of the advantages which the mind draws from it.

This languor and idleness, joined to ignorance, gives rise to a pernicious sensibility, and a desire for public amusements. It also excites an indiscreet and insatiable curiosty.

Persons who are instructed and employed in serious occupations, have generally a moderate degee of curiosity. What they know makes them hold in contempt many things of which they are ignorant. They see the inutility and folly of the greater part of those things which little minds, that know nothing, and that have nothing to do, seek with avidity.

On the contrary, girls ill instructed, and not accustomed to application, have a wandering imagination. For the want of solid nourishment to the mind, their curiosity turns towards objects which are vain and dangerous. Those who have wit, often become conceited, and read books which nourish their vanity; they become passionately fond of romances, of comedies, and of the recital of chimerical adventures, in which profane love is exhibited. These render their minds visionary, in accustoming them to the strained sentiments of romantic heroes; they are even spoiled by this for the world, for all these extravagant sentiments, generous passions, and

wild adventures, which the authors of romances invent to give pleasure, have nothing to do with the motives which govern the actions of men, and which decide their conduct; nor with the disappointments they find in their undertakings.

A poor girl, full of tenderness, and of the marvellous which have charmed her in all she has read, is astonished at not finding in the world persons who resemble her heroes; she would wish to live like those imaginary princesses who, in romances, are always charming, always adored, always above every care. What a disgust for her to descend from a heroine, to the low detail of domestic management! Some push their curiosity still further, and even pretend to judge of religious matters, though they are incapable of it; but she who has not a mind sufficiently enlarged to meddle with these subjects, has others proportioned to her capacity: she ardently desires to know all that is said, or done; a song, a piece of news, an intrigue; to receive letters, to read those which others receive; she will be told every thing, and she tells every thing in return; she is vain, and vanity makes her talk much; she is light, and lightness prevents reflection, which would often keep her silent.

CHAPTER III

WHAT IS THE FIRST FOUNDATION
OF EDUCATION?

O remedy all these evils, it is a great advantage to educate girls from their earliest years. This tender age, which is generally entrusted to servants, who are always ignorant, and often without principle, is that in which the strongest impressions are made, and which is of most importance to the future life.

Before children know how to speak, they may be prepared for instruction. It will be said, that I advance too rapidly; but we have only to consider what children do who cannot yet speak. They learn a language which they will soon utter more intelligibly than the learned, who express themselves in the dead languages which they have studied with so much labor, in the most matured age. But what is it to learn a language? It is not only by selecting in the memory a great number of words; it is, says St. Augustine, by observing the sense of these words in particular. A child, says he, in the midst of its cries and its plays, remarks the object of which each word is the sign, and soon becomes acquainted with them from the different movements of the body of the speaker, which denote the objects spoken of; sometimes being struck by the repetition of the same words signifying the same object. It is true, that the temperament of the brain of children gives them an admirable facility for the impression of all these images. But is not attention of mind required, to discern and to attach each to its separate object?

Consider still further, how much children of this age seek those who flatter them, and shun those who restrain them; they know when to cry, or to be quiet, in order to obtain what they want; they have already acquired artifice and jealousy. I have seen, says St. Augustine, a child, not yet capable of speaking, subject to jealousy, with a pale face and irritated eye, excited to envy against the infant which was nourished at the same breast with itself.

We may then reckon that children know, from this early period, more than is generally imagined; thus you may give them by words, aided by tones and gestures, the inclination of being with worthy and virtuous persons, rather than with those who are irrational, and whom they might be in danger of loving. You may also, by the different forms of your countenance, and by the tone of your voice, give them a horror of those whom they have seen in anger, or in any other way given up to passion; and, by taking a tone more soft, and a countenance more serene, represent to their admiration those whom they have seen behave with wisdom and modesty.

I do not mention these examples as of importance; but to show that these distant indications are beginnings which ought not to be neglected, and this manner of preparing children from their infancy, insensibly facilitates their education. If any yet doubt of the power which these first prejudices of infancy have on manhood, they have only to recollect how much the remembrance of those things which they loved in their childhood, is still lively and touching in advanced age. If, then, instead of giving to children vain fears of phantoms and of spirits, which serve but to weaken and bewilder their understandings, yet tender from the softness of their brain; if, instead of suffering them to follow the imaginations of their nurses for the things which they teach them to love or hate, we endeavored to give them pleasing ideas of excellence, and fearful ideas of evil, this prepossession would greatly facilitate the practice of all virtues.

On the contrary, they are made to fear a priest clothed in black; they speak of death to alarm them; they are told that death comes to them in the night under some fearful form: all this tends but to render their minds weak, and prejudiced against the best things.

To watch the health of children is most useful in the years of infancy; to endeavor to keep the blood pure by the choice of food, and by a simple and regular life; to be careful that their meals are always at the same hour, that they eat sufficiently often for their wants, and that they do not eat between meals, lest the stomach be loaded before digestion. Let them eat nothing highly seasoned, which excites a desire to eat beyond necessity; or which gives a disrelish to more simple food: nor let them eat a variety of things, which only create a false appetite when hunger has been appeased.

It is of still greater consequence to strengthen the organs of the mind, before you oppress them with too much instruction; to avoid every thing which may excite the passions; accustom the child easily to give up those things which it ardently seeks, in order that it may not entertain the hope of possessing every thing which it desires.

Howsoever mischievous the child's natural disposition may be, it is yet easy to render it docile, patient, firm, gay, and even tranquil; whereas, if it be neglected in its infancy, it becomes from thence self-willed, impetuous, and restless all its life. The blood heats, the habits form; the body, yet weak and tender, and the mind, not having acquired a bent towards any particular object, ply themselves towards whatever is evil, and make to themselves a sort of second original sin, which is the source of a thousand disorders in maturer age.

When they arrive at a more advanced period, when reason becomes more developed, it is then necessary that in all our instructions we should inspire them with a love of truth, and a contempt for all dissimulation. Thus we should never make use of any artifice to appease, or persuade them to do what we wish, for by this we would teach them a sort of cunning which they never forget. We ought to lead them, as much as possible, only by reason.

But let us examine the state of children a little more closely, in order to see more particularly what regards them. The substance of their brain is soft, and it becomes harder every day; as to their minds, they know nothing. Every thing is new to them. This softness of the brain makes them receive any impression, and the surprise of novelty creates in them a curiosity, and a desire for admiration. It is true, also, that this softness or humidity of the brain, joined to a great heat, gives them an easy and continual motion: from this arises that agitation of children, which prevents their minds from dwelling upon any object, or their bodies from remaining in any one place.

On the other hand, children, not knowing how to seek, or think, or do any thing of themselves, remark every thing, and speak little if they be not accustomed to speak much; and this should be well guarded against.

The pleasure we derive from pretty and engaging children, spoils them; they are encouraged by it to speak all that enters their mind, and of things of which they have no distinct knowledge. The effect of which is, that there remains with them for life, the habit of judging with precipitation, and of speaking of things of which they have no clear ideas: which stamps a bad character on the mind.

The entertainment which we derive from children, produces another bad effect upon them; they perceive that we notice them, that we observe all they do, that we hear them with pleasure: they are thus accustomed to believe that every body is occupied with them.

During this age wherein they are applauded, and in which they experience no contradiction, they are apt to acquire chimerical hopes, which prepare infinite disappointments for life. I have seen children who believed we spoke of them every time we conversed in secret, because they had observed that we frequently spoke of them; they imagine that every thing in them is extraordinary and admirable. Children should be watched and guarded without perceiving it. Show them that it is from friendship, and from the need they have of your aid, that you are attentive to their conduct, and not from admiration of their talents. Content yourself with forming them by degrees, according as occasions may offer; and

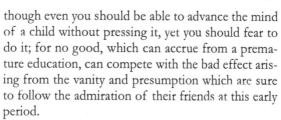

though even you should be able to advance the mind of a child without pressing it, yet you should fear to do it; for no good, which can accrue from a premature education, can compete with the bad effect arising from the vanity and presumption which are sure to follow the admiration of their friends at this early period.

We must content ourselves to follow, and assist nature. Children should not be excited to talk; but as they are ignorant, and know little, they have consequently many questions to ask. It is sufficient to answer them precisely, and sometimes to add little comparisons, in order to render your meaning clearer to them. If they judge of things without understanding them, it may be well to embarrass them by putting some new questions, which will make them feel their fault, without rudely confounding them; at the same time they should be made to feel, not by vague praises, but by some effectual mark of esteem, that they give more satisfaction when they doubt, and when they ask what they do not know, than when they decide correctly. It is the surest means of implanting in their minds a politeness mixed with true modesty, and a disinclination for those contests which are so common amongst young persons not well enlightened.

As soon as it shall appear that their reason has made some progress, we must make use of their experience to fortify them against presumption. You see, you will say to them, that you are more reasonable than you were a year ago; in another year you will know many more things than you do at present. If, a year ago, you had pretended to judge of those things which you now know, but of which you were then ignorant, you would have judged erroneously. You would have been wrong in attempting to decide upon things of which you were ignorant. It is the same now with regard to subjects, of which you have yet to acquire a knowledge. You will one day see how very imperfect your present judgment is. You must therefore, at present, confide in the counsels of those who now judge as you will yourself, when you have attained their age and experience.

The curiosity of children is an inclination of nature which takes the lead of instruction. Do not fail to profit by it. For example, in the country they see a mill, and they wish to know what it is; let them then see how the food is prepared with which man is nourished. When they see reapers, explain to them what they are; how the seed is sown, and how it multiplies in the earth. In the city they see shops, where many arts are exercised, and where many things are sold. You must not be importuned with their questions. Testify only, that you take pleasure in them, and nature will give you openings to facilitate your instructions; by this means they will insensibly become acquainted with every thing which serves for the use of man, and on which commerce depends. By degrees, and without particular study, they will know how to make, in the best manner, all those things which they want for their own use; and the just price of every thing, which is the true foundation of economy. This knowledge, which ought not to be despised by any one, since we all desire not to be deceived in the articles of our expenses, is principally necessary to girls.

CHAPTER IV.

IMITATIONS TO BE FEARED.

 HE ignorance of children, whose minds are free from any impression, and who have not acquired the habit of application, renders them pliant, and inclines them to imitate every thing they see. It is, for this reason, of the utmost importance to propose to them only good models. None should be suffered to approach them except those whose example is proper to be followed. But as it is impossible that they should not sometimes see, in spite of all the precautions which can be taken, many things which are improper, it is necessary to make them remark, at an early age, the impertinence of certain vicious and unreasonable persons, whose characters require no respect. We should show them how much these persons are despised, how much they deserve to be so, and how miserable they are, who give themselves up to their passions, and who do not cultivate their reason. You may thus, without accustoming them to mockery, form their taste, and render them sensible to true benevolence. You should not abstain from pointing out to them generally such kind of defects, lest it should open their eyes to the weaknesses of those whom you would wish them to respect, for we cannot hope, nor would it be just to bring them up in ignorance of true principles on this subject: on the other hand, the surest means of keeping them to their duty, is to persuade them that they must bear with the defects of others, and that they must not even judge of them rashly; that men often appear greater than they are; that these defects are made up for by their good qualities; and that as nothing is perfect on earth, we ought to admire what has the least of imperfection. But however we may reserve these instructions for an extreme case, it is yet necessary to give them just principles, and to guard them, as much as possible, from imitating the evil which they see before them.

We should also prevent their mimicking ridiculous persons; as this habit of acting like a comedian has something in it which is low, and contrary to modesty and good breeding. It is to be feared lest children should acquire this habit, because the warmth of their imaginations, and the pliability of their bodies, joined to their sprightliness, make them easily take all kinds of forms, in order to represent what they see ridiculous.

The inclination which children have for imitation, produces a great number of evils especially where they are under the direction of persons who are not governed by principles of virtue, and who do not restrain themselves before them. But God has given to children this pliability, in order that we may the more easily lead them to what is good. Often without speaking to them, we need only show them in others what we wish them to do.

CHAPTER V.

INDIRECT INSTRUCTION. CHILDREN OUGHT NOT TO BE PRESSED TO RECEIVE INSTRUCTION.

 BELIEVE we might often make use of these indirect instructions, which are much less tiresome to children than lessons and remonstrances, merely to awaken their attention to the examples which we would wish to give them.

A person might sometimes ask another before them: Why do you do that? and the other might reply, I do it for such and such reasons. For example: Why have you confessed your fault? Because I should have committed a much greater one, had I told a lie to hide it; and I think nothing is more beautiful than to say openly, I have been wrong. After this, the first speaker might praise the one who had thus accused himself. But all this must pass naturally without affectation, for children are much more penetrating than people imagine; and from the moment

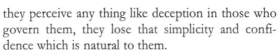

they perceive any thing like deception in those who govern them, they lose that simplicity and confidence which is natural to them.

We have remarked that the brain of children is always warm and humid, and that this causes in them a continual motion. This softness of the brain makes every thing take an easy impression upon it; consequently the images of all sensible objects are there very lively. We should therefore lose no time to imprint on their minds those characters which are so easily formed there. But we must choose images which we would wish to impress upon them; for we would not shut up in a reservoir, so small and so precious, any but exquisite things.

It is to be remembered that we should throw nothing into the minds, at this tender age, but what we would desire to remain there during life. The first images engraved on the mind, while the brain is yet soft, and before any thing else is written there, are the most durable. They harden in proportion as age dries the brain; thus they become ineffaceable. It is for this reason that we so distinctly recollect, when we are old, the things which have happened to us in our youth, however distant the period may be, rather than those which have happened in a more advanced age; because the traces of these were made in the brain when it was already dry, and full of other images.

When we hear this reasoning, we are inclined to

think that it is not just. It is, nevertheless, true, that we reason thus without being aware of it. Do we not say to ourselves every day: My character is formed; I am too old to change; I was brought up in this way of thinking? Besides, do we not feel a particular pleasure in recalling to our minds the images of our youth? Are not our strongest inclinations those which we imbibed at that age? Does not all this prove that the first impressions and habits are the strongest? If then infancy be the time to impress images on the brain, it must be acknowledged that it is not the best for reasoning. This humidity, which renders the impressions so easy, joined to a great heat, gives an agitation which prevents continued application.

The brain of a child is like a lighted taper exposed to the wind, being always glimmering. The child puts a question to you, and before you have answered it, his eyes are raised towards the ceiling, he counts all the figures which are painted there, or all the panes of glass in the window: if you would drive him back to his first object, you restrain him as if you were to imprison him. It is therefore necessary to manage these organs with great care, whilst they are acquiring strength: answer quickly and shortly his questions, and leave him to ask others according to his inclination. Satisfy his curiosity, and let the memory amass for itself a store of good materials. The time will come when he will assemble them; his brain having more consistency, he will be able to follow a continued reasoning. You must forbear to correct him though he should not reason justly; and you should make him feel, without eagerness, as he may give you occasion, how to draw a right inference.

Suffer then a child to play, and mix instruction with it: let wisdom appear to him at intervals, and always with a smiling face. Be careful not to fatigue him by an indiscreet exactness.

If a child take up a dark and sullen view of virtue; if liberty and disorder present themselves to him under agreeable figures, all is lost; your work is vain; never suffer him to be flattered by persons of little understanding, or of irregular conduct. We should accustom ourselves to love the manners and the sentiments of those whom we esteem; the pleasure which we at first experience from persons of ill conduct, makes us, by little and little, come to esteem that which is to be despised.

To render worthy persons agreeable to children, make them remark whatever amiable or accommodating qualities they may have; their sincerity, their modesty, their disinterestedness, their fidelity, their discretion; but, above all, their piety, which is the source of all the rest.

If one amongst them have any thing disgusting about him, say that piety does not give these faults, but that it takes them away when it is perfect; or at least it softens them; after all, we must not obstinately persist in making children like persons who may be good and pious, but whose exterior is disagreeable. Though you may watch over yourself, that nothing may be seen in you but what is good, yet you must not expect the child will never find any fault in you; he will frequently find out even your lightest faults.

St. Augustine tells us that he had remarked, from his infancy, the vanity of his master in his studies. It is most important that you should know your faults, as well as the child will know them; and that you desire your best friends to point them out to you. Generally, those who govern children pardon nothing in them, though they pardon every thing in themselves. This excites in the children a spirit of criticism and of malignity; consequently, when they discover any fault in their governors they are delighted, and feel only contempt for them.

Avoid this inconvenience; fear not to speak of those defects which are visible in yourself, and of those which may have escaped you in the presence of the child. If you see him capable of understanding reason on this point, say that you would give him the example of correcting his faults, as you can correct yours. By this means, you will draw instruction from your faults, and edify the child by encouraging him to correct himself; and you will avoid that

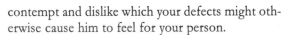

contempt and dislike which your defects might otherwise cause him to feel for your person.

At the same time, it is necessary to find out every
means of rendering agreeable to the child those
things which you exact of him; and should you have
any thing painful to propose, make him understand
that the pain will be followed by pleasure. Always
show him the utility of what you teach him. Make the
usefulness appear with regard to your intercourse
with the world, and the duties of your station.
Without this, study will appear to him an abstracted
labor, barren and full of difficulties. Of what use is it,
he will say to himself, to learn all these things, of
which no one speaks in conversation, and which have
nothing to do with our daily occupations? It is therefore necessary to give him a reason for all the things
which you teach him. You should say to him: It is to
make you more capable of doing what you will have
to do one day or other; to form your judgment, and
to accustom you to reason well upon all the affairs of
life. You should always give to children a solid and
agreeable end to the objects which you hold out to
their view, in order to encourage them in their work,
and never pretend to subject them by a dry and
absolute authority.

In proportion as their reason augments, it will
be well to converse with them more and more on the
necessity of their education; not that it should be the

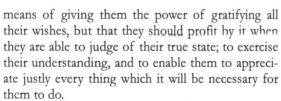

means of giving them the power of gratifying all their wishes, but that they should profit by it when they are able to judge of their true state; to exercise their understanding, and to enable them to appreciate justly every thing which it will be necessary for them to do.

Never assume, without the greatest necessity, an austere or imperious air, which always frightens children, and often arises from affectation and pedantry in those who govern; for children are generally too timid and bashful. You close their hearts from you by it, and make them withdraw their confidence, without which no good fruit can spring from any education. Make yourself beloved by them, and they will be open with you; and they will not fear to let you see their faults. In order to succeed with them, be not too severe to those which they do not disguise from you. Do not appear astonished or irritated at their bad dispositions; on the contrary, be compassionate to their weakness; sometimes this inconvenience will arise from too much lenity, that they will be less withheld by fear; but generally confidence and sincerity are more useful to them, than to exercise a rigorous authority over them.

On the other hand, authority will not fail to find its place, if confidence and persuasion are not sufficiently effectual; but you should begin by an open, gay, and familiar conduct, without meanness; which gives you the opportunity of seeing children act in their natural state, and of knowing their characters thoroughly. If, after all, you should have reduced them by authority to observe all your rules, you would not have gained your end; every thing would become restrained formality, and perhaps hypocrisy. You would disgust them with that good, with a love of which you should alone seek to inspire them.

If the wise say that a parent should always hold the rod over children; if they say that the father who joins in the sports of his child, will weep with him in the end, it is not because they blame an education supported by gentleness and patience. They condemn only those weak and inconsiderate parents, who flatter the passions of their children, and who seek only to divert themselves with them during their infancy, by indulging them in all sorts of excesses. The conclusion to be drawn from this is, that parents should always preserve the authority which gives them the power of correcting, for there are some dispositions which must be governed by fear; but I must repeat, this should only be used when no other means will answer.

A child who acts only from his imagination, and who confounds in his mind all the ideas connected with those who present them, hates study and virtue, because he is prejudiced against the person who proposes them to him.

From this proceeds that idea of piety, so dismal and so frightful, which is frequently retained during life: often is this all that remains of a severe education. It is frequently necessary to tolerate things which ought to be corrected, until the moment shall have arrived when the mind of the child will be in a state to profit by the correction. Never find fault with him in his first emotion, or in yours; if you do it in yours, he will perceive that you are governed by humor and impatience, and not by reason and friendship: you will lose, without resource, your authority. If you reprimand him in his first emotion, his mind will not be sufficiently free to acknowledge his fault, to overcome his passion, and to feel the importance of your advice. It is even exposing the child to lose the respect he owes you. Show him always that you have command over yourself; nothing will make him see it better than your patience. Watch every moment, even though it should be during some days, to correct properly. Do not tell the child his fault, without adding some means by which he may get the better of it, which will encourage him to do so; for we should avoid the discouragement which arises from dry correction. If we find a child somewhat reasonable, I believe it may be well to encourage him gently to ask us to point out his faults; this is a means of pointing them out without giving him pain; and we should never tell him many at a time. It is not to be forgotten that children have weak heads; that their age renders them yet sensible only to pleasure; and that we often demand from them an exactitude and seriousness of which even we ourselves are incapable. We make even a dangerous impression of weariness and sadness on their temperament, by speaking to them always of words and of things which they do not understand: no liberty, no enjoyment, always lessons, silence, restrained posture, correction, and menace.

The ancients understood the treatment of children much better: it was by the pleasures of poetry and music, that the principal sciences, the maxims of virtue, politeness and good manners were introduced among the Hebrews, Egyptians, and Greeks. Those who are not well read, will scarcely believe this; it is totally contrary to our customs; but whoever has even a slight knowledge of history, will know that this was the common practice for many ages. Let us, however, confine ourselves to our own customs, in order to join the agreeable with the useful as much as we can. But though we can hardly hope to succeed always without employing fear with ordinary children, whose dispositions are hard and indocile, we must not have recourse to it till we have patiently tried all other means. It is necessary, however, always to make children understand what we require of them, and with what we shall be content; for joy and confidence must be their ordinary disposition, otherwise we shall

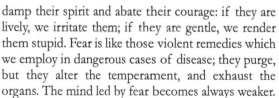

damp their spirit and abate their courage: if they are lively, we irritate them; if they are gentle, we render them stupid. Fear is like those violent remedies which we employ in dangerous cases of disease; they purge, but they alter the temperament, and exhaust the organs. The mind led by fear becomes always weaker.

We must not, on the other hand, always threaten without punishing, lest we give them a contempt for our menaces. We should, however, chastise them less than we threaten; as for chastisement, the pain should be as light as possible, but accompanied by all the circumstances which may affect the child with shame and remorse. For example, show him all you have done to avoid this extremity; appear afflicted by it; speak before him to others of the misfortune of those who are void both of reason and honor, so that it becomes necessary to chastise them; withdraw from him your usual marks of friendship, until you see that he has need of consolation; make this chastisement public, or secret, according as you shall judge it may be most useful to the child, either to cause him a great degree of shame, or to show him that you will spare him from it. Reserve this public shame as a last resource; make use sometimes of a reasonable person to console the child, who may say to him what you could not then say yourself; who will relieve him from his false shame, who will dispose him to return to you, and to whom the child, in his

first emotion, can open his heart more freely than he
would be able to do to you. But above all things, do
not let it appear to the child that you demand from
him unnecessary submissions; endeavor to induce
him to condemn himself, that he may make them
with a good grace, and that it may only remain with
you to soften the pain which he will feel in making
them. Every one must employ these general rules
according to his particular wants. Men, and still less
children, do not always resemble themselves; what is
good to-day may be dangerous to-morrow; and
invariably uniform conduct may not be sometimes
useful. The less we give children of set lessons the
better; we can insinuate a great amount of instruction, more useful even than lessons, in gay conversations. I have known many children who learned a
good deal whilst they were at play; this is done by
recounting to them some entertaining matter which
we take from a book in their presence, and by teaching them insensibly their letters. After this, they will
of themselves wish to find the source of that which
gives them so much pleasure.

There are two things which spoil every thing.
The first is, when we make them begin to learn to
read Latin, which takes away all the pleasure of reading; and also when we accustom them to read with an
affected and ridiculous emphasis. We should give
them books well ornamented, even on the outside,

with the most beautiful pictures, and characters well formed; every thing which pleases the imagination facilitates study. We should endeavor to choose books full of short and wonderful histories; this done, be not in trouble about the child's learning to read correctly. Let him pronounce naturally as he speaks: other tones are always bad; it partakes of the declamation of a college: when his tongue shall be pliable, and his lungs stronger, and the habit of reading greater, he will read without difficulty, more gracefully and more distinctly.

The manner of teaching to write ought to be nearly the same. When a child already knows how to read a little, we may make it a diversion for him to form letters; and if there are many together, you may cause an emulation amongst them. Children of their own accord will apply themselves to make figures on paper; if we assist this inclination a little, without restraining them too much, they will form letters as they play, and accustom themselves by degrees to write. We may even excite them by promising them some recompense which will be to their taste, but which will not have any dangerous consequence.

Write me a note, you may say to the child; ask something for your brother or your cousin; all this gives pleasure to the child, provided no dull images or regulated lessons be found in it to trouble him. A free curiosity, says St. Augustine from his own experience, excites much more the mind of a child, than a rule and a necessity imposed through fear.

Let us here remark a great defect in the common modes of education. We put all the pleasure on one side, and all the weariness on the other. The weariness on that of study, the pleasure on that of diversion. What can a child do, but support with impatience the task, and run ardently after play?

Let us then endeavor to change this order; let us render study agreeable; let us hide it under the appearance of liberty and pleasure. Let us suffer the children to interrupt the study by little sallies of diversion; they have need of these wanderings to refresh their minds.

Suffer them to walk about a little; permit them even now and then some digression, or some play, that their minds may be set at large; then bring them back gently to the task. Too much regularity, in exacting from them an uninterrupted application to study, hurts them much; those who govern often affect this regularity, because it is more convenient to themselves, than subjecting themselves continually to profit by the moments which offer.

At the same time, we must take from children all those diversions which too much excite their passions; all that can refresh their mind, all that can offer an agreeable variety to them, that can satisfy their curiosity for useful things, that can exercise their bodies to agreeable arts; all these should be employed in the diversions of children. Those which they like better keep the body in motion; they are content, provided they often change place; a shuttlecock or a bowl is sufficient. Thus, it is not necessary to be in trouble about their amusements, they will invent new ones themselves; all that is required is to suffer them to act, to observe them with a gay countenance, and to moderate them as soon as they become overheated. It is good simply to make them feel, as much as possible, the pleasures which the mind derives from conversation, from anecdotes, from several ingenious histories which contain much instruction. All this must be used according to the occasion; but the taste of the child must not be forced; we should only offer the opportunity to him to exercise it; some days the body will be less disposed to move about, and the mind will be more active.

The care which we should take to season serious occupations with pleasure, will serve much to abate the ardor of youth for dangerous pleasures. It is subjection and weariness which give such an impatient desire for diversion. If a girl felt less tired in the company of her mother she would not wish so much to escape from her, to seek other company, perhaps not so good for her.

In the choice of diversions, all suspected societies should be avoided. No boys with girls, nor should girls even be introduced whose minds are not well directed. Plays which dissipate, and which excite passion too much, or which occasion an agitation of the body, which would not be modest for girls, frequently going from home, and conversations which give only desire of going from home, ought to be avoided. When we are not spoiled by any great diversions, and when no ardent passion has taken possession of us, we easily find pleasure. Health and innocence are its true sources; but those who have had the misfortune to accustom themselves to violent pleasures, lose all taste for those of a more moderate nature, and fatigue themselves in a restless pursuit after such as serve only to dissipate the mind.

We spoil our taste for pleasure as for food; we accustom ourselves to high-flavored dishes, till those which are simple and unseasoned become flat and insipid. Let us then fear those great emotions of the mind which lead to weariness and disgust; but above all, they are to be feared for those children who never resist their feelings, and who are always seeking emotion. Let us give them a taste for simple things; it does not require much food to nourish them, nor great preparations to entertain them and give them pleasure. Moderation always gives sufficient appetite, without having recourse to delicacies, which cause intemperance. Temperance, said an ancient writer, is the best workman for voluptuousness. With this temperance, which produces health of body and mind, we always feel a sweet and moderate joy; we neither require public shows, nor expense to enjoy ourselves; a little play which we invent, reading a good book, some work which we undertake, a walk for amusement, an innocent conversation which refreshes after labor, makes us feel a purer joy than the most delightful music.

Simple pleasures are less lively and less sensible, it is true; others carry away the mind in shaking the spring of the passions, but simple pleasures are the best; they give an equal and lasting joy, without leaving any hurtful impression. They are always beneficial; whereas other pleasures are like adulterated wines, which please at first more than the pure wine; but which alter and hurt the constitution: the temperament of the mind spoils itself as much as the taste by this research after lively and studied pleasures. All that we can do for the children whom we govern, is to accustom them to this simple life, to fortify them by it, as long as we can to forewarn them by fear of the inconveniences attached to other pleasures, and not to abandon them to themselves, as is generally done, at the age when the passions begin to be felt, and when, consequently, they have more need of being restrained.

Of all the troubles of education, none are to be compared to that of bringing up a child who wants sensibility. Lively and sensitive dispositions are capable of great wanderings. Passion and presumption lead them on; but they have great resources, and often return from error. Instruction is in them a hidden germ, which shoots out and fructifies, sometimes when experience comes to the assistance of reason, and when the passions cool; besides we know by what means to render them attentive, and to awaken their curiosity. You find in them sufficient to enable you to interest them in what you wish to teach them, and to offend their honor; whereas you have no hold upon an indolent person. All the thoughts of such are distracting, they never are where they ought to be; you cannot even move them much by correction; they hear all, but feel nothing. This indolence renders the child negligent and disgusted with every thing he does; then it is that the best education runs the risk of being thrown away, if we do not hasten to check the evil from the earliest infancy. Many persons who do not reflect deeply, conclude from this ill success, that every thing depends on nature in forming the man of merit, and that education has nothing to do in it; whereas the only conclusion to draw is, that there are some dispositions which resemble an ungrateful soil, on which culture does but little. It is still worse when these troublesome characters are crossed, or neglected, or ill regulated in the commencement.

It is also to be observed, that there are children
in whose dispositions we are greatly deceived. They
appear at first pretty, because the first graces of infancy have a lustre which cover every thing. We see in
them every thing that is tender and amiable, which
prevents our examining more closely the more
minute traits of their countenance. All that we find in
their mind surprises us, because we do not expect it at
this age. All the faults of judgment are permitted, and
have the grace of ingenuity; we take a certain vivacity
of the body, which never fails to appear in children,
for that of the mind. Hence it is that infancy seems to
promise so much, and gives so little. Such a one has
been celebrated for his wit until the age of five years,
but afterwards has fallen into obscurity and contempt
in proportion as he grew up. Of all the qualities
which we see in children, there is only one on which
we can depend—it is the faculty of reasoning; it
grows always with them, provided it be well cultivated. The graces of infancy wear out, vivacity extin-
guishes itself, tenderness of heart is even sometimes
lost, because their passions and the dangerous intercourse with men insensibly harden the hearts of
young persons on entering into the world. Endeavor
then to discover if the temper you have to govern be
wanting in curiosity, and if it be insensible to honest
emulation. In this case, it will be difficult for those
charged with his education not to be soon repulsed

by a labor so ungrateful and thorny. Here it is necessary to stir up all the resources of the soul of the child, to draw him out of his lethargy. If you foresee this inconvenience, do not at first press a formal course of instruction; take great care not to overcharge his memory, for it is this which stuns and weighs down the brain. Do not fatigue him by restrained rules: enliven him, if he fall into the extreme contrary to presumption; do not fear to show him, with discretion, of what he is capable; content yourself with little; make him remark his most trifling success; represent to him how unfounded were his fears that he would not succeed in what he had done well; put him on a work of emulation. Jealousy is more violent in children than we imagine; we see them sometimes, from it, shutting up their minds, and wasting with a secret languor, because others are more loved and more caressed. It is a cruelty, too common with mothers, to let them suffer this torment; but it may be well to employ this remedy, on the most pressing occasions, against indolence. Put before the child whom you bring up, other children who are but a little more forward than himself. Examples too much disproportioned to his weakness would but discourage him.

Give him, from time to time, little victories over those with whom he is jealous; engage him to laugh freely with you at his timidity; show him others like himself, who got the better of this defect of their constitution; teach him, by indirect instructions with regard to others, that timidity and idleness stifle the spirit; that persons who are lazy, and without application, whatever genius they may have, become imbecile and degraded; but take good care not to give these instructions in an austere or impatient tone, for nothing so much shuts up the mind of a child, who is dull and timid, as harshness: on the contrary, redouble your care to season, and to make the labor which you cannot spare him, easy and pleasant, in proportion to his natural disposition. Perhaps it will be necessary, from time to time, to rouse him by contempt and reproach. You must not do it yourself; but some one inferior, as another child, may do it without your appearing to know it.

St. Augustine relates, that a reproach made to Saint Monica his mother, in her infancy, by a servant, touched her so much as to induce her to leave off a bad habit which she had acquired, of drinking pure wine, which the vehemence and severity of her governess had not had the power of doing. In short, we must endeavor to give taste to the minds of children of this disposition, as we give it to the palate of certain invalids. We suffer them to seek whatever may cure their incapacities; we suffer in the children some humor, at the expense even of rules, provided that they be not carried to a dangerous excess. It is more difficult to give taste to those who have it not, than to form that of those who have not already such as it ought to be.

Another kind of sensibility, still more difficult and more important, is that of friendship. From the moment a child is capable of this, there is no fear but his heart may be turned towards those persons who will be useful to him. Friendship will lead him towards every thing that we may desire; we have a certain tie upon him which will attract him towards goodness, provided we know how to make use of it. There remains nothing to be feared but an excess, or a bad choice in his affections. But there are other children who are born politicians, artful, and with an apparent indifference, yet desirous to draw every thing secretly to themselves; they deceive their parents, whom tenderness renders credulous; they pretend to love them; they study their inclinations in order to conform to them; they appear more docile than other children of the same age, who act without disguise according to their humor; their subtlety, which hides their self-will, appears to be nothing but gentleness, and their natural dissimulation does not wholly display itself, till there is no longer time to redress it.

If there be children upon whose dispositions education can do nothing, these are they. It must, however, be confessed, that their number is much greater than we imagine. Parents cannot believe that their children have bad hearts; and when they will not see it, no one wishes to convince them of it; and the evil must always increase. The principal remedy would be to give such children, from their infancy, an entire liberty of displaying their inclination. We must always know them well, before we correct them. Children are naturally simple and open; but if we restrain them ever so little, or give them the smallest example of disguise, they never return to their first simplicity. It is true that God alone gives tenderness and goodness of heart; we can only endeavor to excite it by generous examples, by honorable maxims, by disinterestedness, and by showing contempt for those people who have too much self-love. It is necessary to make children taste, at an early age, before they have lost their first simplicity, by emotions the most natural, the pleasure of a cordial and reciprocal friendship. Nothing will answer this purpose so well, as to place persons who never show any harsh, false, low, or interested treatment, near them. It would be better to place about them those who have other faults, but who are exempt from these. We should also praise children for every thing which they do from friendship, provided it be not out of place, or too ardent. Their parents should also appear full of sincere friendship for them; for children often learn, even from their parents, to love nothing. In short, I would withhold from them, with regard to friends, all

superfluous compliments, all pretended demonstra-
tions of regard, and all false caresses, by which we
may teach them to make vain appearance towards
persons whom they ought to love.

There is another fault the opposite to this which
we have represented, that is more common amongst
girls. It is that of being passionately fond of even the
most indifferent things. They cannot see two persons
who differ with one another, without taking part in
their hearts for one side or the other; they are full of
affection, or aversion, but without foundation; they
perceive no defect in those whom they esteem, and
no good quality in those whom they dislike. We must
not at first oppose them, for contradiction strength-
ens these fancies; but, by little and little, we must
make young people remark that we know better than
they do, all the good of those whom they love, and all
the evil of those whom they hate. Take care, at the
same time, to make them feel on these occasions the
inconveniences of the defects which will be found in
the person who charms them, and the convenience
arising from the advantageous qualities which we
meet with in the one who gives them displeasure. Do
not press the subject too much, for you will soon see
that they will return to themselves. After this, make
them remark their first infatuation, with the most
unreasonable circumstances belonging to it. Tell
them gently that they will see, in the same manner, the

prepossessions of which they are not yet cured, when they shall be at an end. Tell them of the same errors of which you were guilty at their age. Above all, show them, in the clearest manner that you can, the great mixture of good and evil which we find in all those whom we may love or hate, in order to slacken the ardor of their friendships and their aversions.

Never promise to give children, as a recompense, either articles of dress or good things to eat: for this would be causing two evils, the first by inspiring them with an esteem for what they ought to despise, and the second by taking from you the means of establishing other recompenses which would facilitate your work. Take good care never to threaten them with any thing to study, nor to subject them to any rules. We should make as few rules as possible, and when they cannot be avoided; we should exercise them gently, without giving them the name of rules, and showing always some sufficient reason for doing the thing at this time, and in this place, rather than in another. We run the risk of discouraging children, if we never praise them when they do well. Though praises are to be feared on account of vanity, still we must endeavor to make use of them to encourage children, without flattering them.

We see that St. Paul employs praises often to encourage the weak, and to soften correction. The Fathers made the same use of them. It is true, that in order to render them useful, we must adapt them so as to take from them all appearance of exaggeration or flattery, and, at the same time, attribute all the good to God as its source. We can also reward children by permitting them to play at innocent games which require some skill and ingenuity; by walking, when conversation is not without its fruit; by little presents, which will be a sort of prize; such as prints, pictures, medals, maps, or ornamented books.

CHAPTER VI.

ON THE USE OF HISTORY FOR CHILDREN.

HILDREN are passionately fond of wonderful and ridiculous tales; we see them continually transported with joy, or shedding tears, at the recital of adventures which we relate to them. Do not fail to profit by this inclination. When you see them disposed to hear you, recount to them some short and pretty story; but choose some stories about animals which will be ingenious and innocent. As to heathen fables, it is better that girls should be always ignorant of them, because, generally speaking, they are impure, and full of impious absurdities. If you cannot keep them entirely ignorant of them, inspire, as much as possible, a horror of them. When you shall have recounted one story, wait till the child shall ask you for another; his thirst for them being thus awakened, and his curiosity being excited, relate certain select histories, but in few words; connect them together, and put off from day

to day the relation of the sequel, in order to hold the
child in suspense, and to give him an impatience to
know the end; animate your recitals with a lively and
familiar tone; make all your characters speak.
Children who have lively imaginations will believe
that they see and hear what you tell them. For example, relate the history of Joseph to them; make his
brothers speak like savages, Jacob like a tender and
afflicted father; when Joseph himself speaks, let him
take pleasure in being master in Egypt, in keeping
himself unknown to his brothers, to excite their fear,
and then finally to discover himself. This simple representation, joined to the wonders of this history, will
charm the child, provided we do not overload him
with such recitals, and that we leave him free to wish
for them, that we promise them even as a recompense when he acts wisely; that we do not give them
an air of study, nor oblige the child to repeat them.
These repetitions, if they be not their own voluntary
act, restrain the child, and take from him all the pleasure of such stories.

We should, nevertheless, observe whether, if the
child has any facility in repeating, he will of his own
accord repeat, to some person whom he loves, the
histories which have given him most pleasure; but we
should not make a rule of it. You can make use of
some person who will be free with the child, and who
may appear to desire to hear him recite his history.

The child will be delighted to recount it to him. Do not appear to pay any attention; let him do it without being reminded of his faults. Then, when he will be more accustomed to this exercise, you can make him remark gently, the best manner of telling a story, which is to make it short, simple, and agreeable, by the choice of such circumstances as most naturally represent each part. If you have many children, accustom them by degrees to represent the characters of the histories which they have learned; the one will be Abraham, the other Isaac. These representations will charm them more than other plays; they will accustom them to think and to speak of serious things with pleasure, and will render these histories indelibly fixed in their memories.

We should endeavor to give them more taste for sacred history than for any other, not by telling them that these are prettier, which probably they would not believe, but by making them feel it without telling them. Make them remark how important, how singular, how extraordinary, how full of natural pictures, and of a noble vivacity, they are. Those of the creation, of the fall of Adam, of the deluge, of the call of Abraham, of the sacrifice of Isaac, of the adventures of Joseph which we have mentioned, of the birth and the flight of Moses, are not only proper to awaken the curiosity of children, but, in discoursing to them on the origin of religion, to establish its

foundation in their minds. We must be profoundly
ignorant of the essential foundation of religion, not
to see that it is all historical; for it is by a tissue of
extraordinary facts, that we find its establishment, its
perpetuity, and every thing which ought to make us
believe and practise it, supported.

We are not to imagine that we shall be able to
engage young persons to dive deeply into this science,
when we propose to them all these histories, even
though they are short, varied, and adapted to please
the most ignorant. God, who knows better than we do
the mind of man which he has formed, has put religion into popular facts, which, so far from overcharg-
ing the weakest powers, on the contrary assist them to
conceive and to retain its mysteries. For example, say
to a child, that in God three equal persons are but one
single nature. In consequence of hearing and repeating these terms, he will retain them in his memory; but
1 doubt whether he will be able to conceive the sense
of them. Relate to him that when Jesus Christ was
coming out of the waters of Jordan, his Father caused
his voice to be heard from heaven, saying: "This is my
beloved Son, in whom I am well pleased; hear ye him."
Add, that the Holy Ghost descended on him in the
form of a dove. You will make him clearly find the
Trinity in this history, which he will not forget. Behold
here three persons, whom he will always distinguish by
the difference of their actions; you will only have to

teach him, that altogether they are but one God. This example is sufficient to show the utility of such recitals; though they appear to lengthen the instruction, they shorten it much, and take from it the dulness of catechisms, in which the mysteries are detached from the facts. Let us see if the ancients instructed by this means. The admirable manner in which St. Augustine advises the ignorant to be instructed, was not a method which this father introduced; it was the universal method and practise of the church. It consisted in showing, by the succession of history, that religion was as ancient as the world. Belief in Jesus Christ to come, in the Old Testament, and in Jesus Christ reigning in the New, is the foundation of all Christian instruction.

This demands a little more time and care than the instruction to which most persons confine themselves; but then we know religion truly, when we know these details; on the contrary, when we are ignorant of them, we have but confused ideas of Jesus Christ, of the Gospel, the Church, the necessity of submitting ourselves absolutely to its decisions, and the foundation of those virtues with which the name of Christian ought to inspire us. The historical catechism, printed a short time since, which is a short, simple book, and much more clear than the ordinary catechisms, contains all that is necessary to be known on the subject; thus it cannot be said that much study is demanded. This, in its design, is the same as that of the council of Trent, with this circumstance, that the catechism of the council is a little too much mixed with theological terms for simple persons.

Let us then join to the histories which I have remarked, the passage of the Red Sea, and the sojourn of the people in the desert, where they ate bread which fell from heaven, and drank of water which Moses drew from a rock, by striking it with his rod. Represent the miraculous conquest of the promised land, when the waters of the Jordan returned towards their source, and the walls of a city fell of themselves at the sight of the besiegers. Represent to the life the combats of Saul and of David. Show how David, from his youth, without arms, in his shepherd's habit, vanquished the fierce giant, Goliath. Do not forget the glory and the wisdom of Solomon: make him decide between the two women who disputed about the child; but show him falling from the height of his wisdom, and dishonoring himself by voluptuousness, a consequence almost inevitable of too much prosperity.

Make the prophets speak to the kings respecting the will of God; let them read in the future as in a book, let them appear humble, austere, and suffering continual persecutions for having told the truth. Put in its proper place the first ruin of Jerusalem; show the burning of the temple, and the holy city destroyed

on account of the sins of the people. Recount the
captivity of Babylon, where the Jews wept for their
beloved Sion. Before their return, introduce the
delightful adventures of Tobias, and Judith, Esther,
and Daniel. It would not be useless to make the children give an opinion on the different characters of
these saints, to discover those whom they admire
most. One will prefer Esther, another Judith, and this
will excite a little contention between them, which
will impress the history more strongly on their minds,
and form their judgment. Then lead back the people
to Jerusalem, make them repair its ruins; make a smiling picture of peace, and of its happiness; soon after,
draw a portrait of the cruel and impious Antiochus,
who died calling for mercy, but in vain. Show, under
this persecution, the victories of the Maccabees, and
the martyrdom of the seven brothers of that name.
Come to the miraculous birth of St. John. Relate,
more in detail, that of Jesus Christ; after which make
choice, in the Gospel, of all the striking parts of his
life — his preaching in the temple at the age of twelve
years — his baptism — his retreat to the desert, and
his temptation — the vocation of his apostles — the
miracle of the loaves — the conversation of the sin-
ful woman who anointed the feet of our Saviour with
the perfumed ointment, washed them with her tears,
and dried them with her hair. Represent the
Samaritan instructed, the blind cured, Lazarus

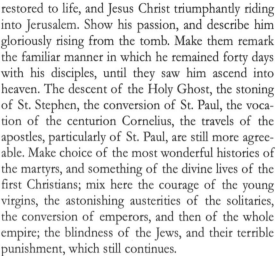

restored to life, and Jesus Christ triumphantly riding into Jerusalem. Show his passion, and describe him gloriously rising from the tomb. Make them remark the familiar manner in which he remained forty days with his disciples, until they saw him ascend into heaven. The descent of the Holy Ghost, the stoning of St. Stephen, the conversion of St. Paul, the vocation of the centurion Cornelius, the travels of the apostles, particularly of St. Paul, are still more agreeable. Make choice of the most wonderful histories of the martyrs, and something of the divine lives of the first Christians; mix here the courage of the young virgins, the astonishing austerities of the solitaries, the conversion of emperors, and then of the whole empire; the blindness of the Jews, and their terrible punishment, which still continues.

All these accounts, managed discreetly, will be received with pleasure into the imaginations of lively and tender children. The whole course of religion, from the creation of the world to the present time, gives noble ideas to them, which will never be effaced. They will even see, in this history, the hand of God always raised to deliver the just, and to confound the impious; they will be accustomed to see God, the author of every thing, secretly leading to his designs, creatures which appear the most distant from him. But it is necessary to collect every thing in these recitals, which may form in the mind the most smil-

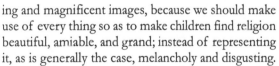

ing and magnificent images, because we should make use of every thing so as to make children find religion beautiful, amiable, and grand; instead of representing it, as is generally the case, melancholy and disgusting.

Besides the inestimable advantage of thus teaching religion to children, the fund of agreeable histories which they thus remember at an early age, awakens their curiosity for serious things—renders them sensible to the pleasures of the mind—and makes them interest themselves when they hear other histories spoken of which have some connexion with those which they already know. But I must repeat, that it is necessary to guard against making it a law for them to hear, or be obliged to remember these recitals, much less to make them regular lessons. Every thing must be done through pleasure. Do not press them; you will obtain your end even with common minds, if you do not overcharge them too much; and if you suffer their curiosity to come by degrees. But you will say, how are we to relate these histories in a lively—short—natural, and agreeable manner; where are the governesses who can do it? To this I answer, that I only propose it; that we should endeavor to find persons of good minds to govern children, and that we should inspire them as much as possible with this method of teaching. Every governess should adopt it according to the extent of her powers. But if they have ever so little enlargement of mind things will go better if we form the children in this simple and natural manner.

You may add to your discourse the sight of prints or pictures, which agreeably represent the sacred histories. Prints may suffice, and we may generally use them; but when we have the opportunity of showing the children good pictures we should not neglect it; for the force of colors, with the grandeur of figures, will strike their imagination more forcibly.

CHAPTER VII.

HOW TO MAKE THE FIRST PRINCIPLES OF RELIGION ENTER INTO THE MINDS OF CHILDREN.

E have remarked, that children in their earliest age are not formed for reasoning. Not that they are without the ideas and general principles of reasoning, which they will finally acquire, but for want of knowing many facts they cannot apply their reason; and on the other hand, the agitation of their brain prevents them from following and connecting their thoughts.

We must, however, without pressing them, gently turn the first use of their reason to the knowledge of God; persuade them of the truths of Christianity, without giving them any subjects of doubt. For instance, they see some one die; they know that he will be buried. Say to them, where is this dead person —is he in the tomb? Yes. He is not then in paradise? Yes he is. How can he be in paradise and in the tomb at the same time? The soul only is in paradise. The

57

body is put in the earth. The soul then is not the body? No. Then the soul is not dead? No; it will always live in heaven. You may add: Do you wish to be saved? Yes. But what means to be saved? That the soul should go into paradise when the body dies. And what is death? The separation of the soul and body, and the return of the body into dust.

I do not pretend to say that we can lead children at first to answer in this manner: I can say, nevertheless, that many have given me these answers at the age of four years. But if we suppose a mind less open, and more retiring, the worst that can happen is, to wait some years longer without impatience.

We should show children a house, and accustom them to learn that this house was not built by itself. The stones, you will tell them, would not have been placed without some person bringing them there. It will be well even to show them some masons who are building: then make them look at the heavens, the earth, and the principal things which God has placed there for the use of man. Then say to them, you see how much more beautiful and better the world is made than any house. Was the world made by itself? No; without doubt, it was God only who could make it.

At first, follow the method of the Scriptures; strike their imaginations in a lively manner, and propose nothing to them which is not clothed in sensible images. Represent God seated on a throne, with eyes more brilliant than the rays of the sun and more piercing than the lightning. Make him speak, give him ears which hear every thing, hands which carry the universe, arms always raised to punish the wicked, and a heart tender and paternal, to render those happy who love him. The time will come when you may render all this knowledge more exact. Observe all the openings which the mind of the child gives you; try every means by which these great truths may the better enter his understanding. Above all, tell him nothing new, without familiarizing it to him by some sensible comparison.

For example, ask him if he would rather die than renounce Jesus Christ, he will answer yes. But would you be willing to give your head to be cut off, to go into paradise? Yes. So far the child believes that he should have sufficient courage to do it; but if you wish to make him feel that we can do nothing without grace, you will gain nothing if you tell him simply that he has need of grace to be faithful; he will not understand the meaning of these words, and if you accustom him to hear them without understanding them, you will not be more advanced. What will you do then? Relate to him the history of St. Peter; represent him saying, in a presumptuous tone: "If you die, I will follow you; though every one else should quit you, I will never abandon you." Then depict his fall; how he denied Christ three times, on account of fear

with which he was inspired by a servant. Tell him why
God permitted him to be so weak; then make use of
the comparison of a child, or of a sick person, who
cannot stand alone, and make him understand that we
have need of God to support us, as a nurse supports
a child; by this you will render the mystery of grace
clear to him.

But the truth most difficult to make him understand, is that we have a soul far more precious than
our body. We accustom children from the beginning
to speak of the soul, and we do well; for this language, which they do not understand, nevertheless
accustoms them to a confused idea of the distinction
between the body and the soul, until the time shall
have arrived when they can understand it. In as much
as the prejudices of children are pernicious when
they lead to error, in so much are they useful when
they accustom the imagination to truth, before reason
can adopt them from principle. But finally, we must
establish a true persuasion. How is this to be done?
Will it be by leading a young girl into the subtleties of
philosophy? Nothing is so bad. We must content ourselves with explaining to her, as clearly and as sensibly
as we can, what she may understand, and what she
says every day.

For her person, she will attend to it but too well;
every thing conduces to flatter her and induce her to
ornament it, and to make it an idol. It is important to

inspire her with contempt for it, by showing her that she has something in her of more worth. Say then to a child, in whom reason begins to act, is it your soul that eats? If she answer ill, do not scold her; but tell her gently that her soul does not eat. It is the body, you will say, that eats, and is like to the beasts. Have the beasts minds? Are they learned? No, the child will reply. But they eat, you will continue, though they have no mind. You clearly see, then, that it is not the mind that eats. It is the body which takes food to nourish it. It is the body that walks, and sleeps. And, what does the soul do? It reasons — it knows every body — it loves certain things, there are others which it regards with aversion. Ask her playfully, do you see this table? Yes. You know it, then? Yes. You see well that it is not made like this chair; you know that it is of wood, and that it is not like the chimney, which is of stone? Yes, the child will reply. Go no further, unless you see in the tones and the eyes of the child, that these simple truths have struck her. Then add, but does this table know you? You will see that she will laugh at the mockery of this question. No matter; ask her, who loves you better than this table, or this chair? She will still laugh. Continue. And the window, is it wise? Then endeavor to go farther. And this doll, will it answer when you speak to it? No. Why not? Is it because it has no mind? Certainly, it has none. It is not then like you, for you know it, and it does not

know you. But, after your death, when you will be in
the earth, will you not be like this doll? Yes. You will
no longer feel any thing? No. And your soul will then
be in heaven? Yes. Will it not see God? True. And the
soul of the doll, where is it at present? You will see
the child laugh in answering you—but at least you will
make her understand that the doll has no soul.

On this foundation, and by these little sensible
images, make use of every renewed occasion, to
accustom the child by degrees to attribute to the body
what belongs to it, and to the soul what comes from
it; provided you do not indiscreetly propose to her
certain actions which are common to both. You must
avoid subtleties which would confound these truths,
and you must content yourself with marking out distinctly those things where the difference of the body
and soul is clearly perceived. Perhaps we may find
minds so gross that, even with a good education, they
will not be able to understand distinctly these truths;
and when we instruct, we may sometimes conceive a
thing very clearly, though we do not always know how
to explain it well; on the other hand, God sees better
than we do, how he has formed the mind of man for
the reception of his mysteries.

For those children in whom we perceive talents
capable of going farther, we can, without involving
them in a philosophical study, make them conceive,
according to the capability of their minds, what we

mean when we tell them that God is a spirit, and that their soul is also a spirit. I believe that the best and simplest means of making them understand this spirituality of God and of the soul is, to make them remark the difference between a dead and a living man: in the one there is nothing but the body; in the other the body is joined to the soul. Afterwards we may show that a being, possessed of reason, is much more perfect than one that is merely capable of motion. Make them also remark, by familiar examples, that nothing perishes. Thus for instance: a piece of wood which is burned becomes ashes or disperses itself in smoke. If then you will say, that which is in itself nothing but dust, incapable of knowing and of thinking, never perishes, how much more reason have we to believe that our souls, which know and think, will never cease to exist? The body can die; that is to say, it can quit the soul and become dust, but the soul will live, for it will always think.

Those who teach ought to impress this kind of knowledge as deeply as possible in the minds of children, for it is the foundation of all religion. But when they cannot succeed, they should, instead of being discouraged by their dulness and stupidity, on the contrary, hope that God will enlighten them. There is even a clear and practical way by which this knowledge of the distinction between body and soul may be increased, and this is to accustom the child to despise the one, and to esteem the other, in all the details of morality. Praise that instruction which nourishes the mind and makes it expand; esteem those grand truths which animate us, and render us wiser and more virtuous. Despise every thing like good living, dress, or whatever else may tend to relax the body. Make a child feel how much honor, a good conscience, and religion, are superior to gross pleasures, by means of such sentiments, without entering on a course of reasoning on the body and the soul. The ancient Romans taught their children to despise the body, and to sacrifice it for the pleasures which the soul received from virtue and glory. Amongst them not only persons of distinguished birth, but even the whole of the people were born temperate — disinterested, full of contempt for this life — sensible only to honor and to wisdom. When I speak of the ancient Romans, I mean those who lived before the power and splendor of their empire had altered the simplicity of their manners.

Let us not say that it would be impossible to give children such prejudices by education. How many maxims do we see established amongst ourselves, against the impressions of our feeling, by force of custom? For example, that of duelling, founded on a false notion of honor. It is not from reasoning, but from adopting without reasoning, the established maxim on the point of honor, that one exposes his life, and that all military men live in continual peril. He who has no quarrel may enter into one at any time with any of those people who only seek an opportunity to signalize themselves in combat. However moderate he may be, he cannot, without losing this false honor, either avoid a quarrel himself, or refuse to be seconds to any one who may request it, and who wishes to fight. As yet no power has been found sufficient to root out a custom so barbarous. See, then, how powerful are the prejudices of education; they will do much more for virtue when they shall be supported by reason, and by the hope of the kingdom of heaven. The Romans, of whom we have already spoken, and before them the Greeks, in the early time of their republic, brought up their children in contempt of ambition and of idleness; they brought them up to esteem one glory, to desire not to possess riches, but to overcome the kings who possessed them, and to believe that they could only be happy by the practice of virtue. This spirit was so strongly established in those republics, that they have done incredible things, according to these maxims, so contrary to those of all other people. The examples of the martyrs, and of others amongst the first Christians, of all conditions and of all ages, clearly show that the grace of baptism, being added to the assistance of education, can make impressions yet more astonishing in the faithful, to induce them to despise what belongs to the body. Seek, then, the most agreeable manner, and the most striking comparisons, to convince children that our bodies are like the beasts, and that our souls are like the angels. Represent a rider mounted on a horse which he guides; say that the soul is, in respect to the body, what this rider is to his horse. Finish by saying that the soul is very weak and very unhappy when it suffers itself to be carried away by the body, as by a furious horse, which throws his rider into a precipice. Make them remark, that beauty of person is like a flower which opens itself in the morning, and at night fades, and is trodden under foot; but that the soul is the image of the immortal God. There is, you will add, an order of things much more excellent, than that which we see with our mortal eyes, for we see every thing here below subject to change and corruption. To make children feel that there are things real, which the eyes and the ears cannot perceive, we should demand of them if it be not true that such a person is wise, and that such another has great wit? When they shall have answered yes, you will ask them: Have you ever seen the wisdom of that person? Of what color is it? Have you ever heard it? Does it make much noise? Have you touched it? Is it cold or hot? The child will laugh; he will do so when asked the same questions on the mind; he will appear quite astonished that we should ask him of what color is his mind; whether it be round or square. Thus, you may make him remark that he knows things which are very true, but which he can neither see, nor touch, nor hear, and that those things are spiritual. But we must enter very cautiously upon these discourses with girls. I propose them here only for those whose curiosity and reason lead you, in spite of yourself, to these questions. We must be guided according to the opening of their minds, and according to their wants.

Keep their minds, as much as you can, within common bounds, and teach them that their sex should feel a modesty with regard to science, almost as delicate as that which would inspire them with a horror of vice.

At the same time we should bring the imagination to aid the understanding, to give them charming images of the truth of religion, which would not be seen without this help. We should paint to them celestial glory, such as St. John represents it to us; all tears dried up; no more death; no more grief or cries; no sighs will escape us; all evil will be passed away; an eternal joy will flow over the hearts of the blessed, as the waters flow over the head of a man immersed in the depth of the sea. Show that glorious Jerusalem, of which God will himself be the sun, to light the days without end, in one uninterrupted flow of peace, in a torrent of delights, where we shall be refreshed by the waters of the fountain of life, where all will be gold, pearls, and precious stones. I well know that all these images attach to sensible things; but after having awakened the children by a spectacle so beautiful, in order to render them attentive, we must make use of these means, which we have already touched, to lead them to things spiritual.

Conclude by saying, that we are only on this earth like travellers in a hotel, or under a tent; that the body will perish, that we can retard its corruption only a few years, but that the soul will take its flight to that celestial country where it will live forever as God lives. If we could give children the habit of looking with pleasure upon these grand objects, and of judging of common things in comparison of these high hopes, we should smooth infinite difficulties.

I would also endeavor to give them strong impressions on the resurrection of the body. Teach them that nature is subject to the common order which God has established in his works, that miracles are only exceptions to his general rules, and that it costs God no more to perform a hundred miracles, than it costs me to go out of my chamber a quarter of an hour sooner than I am accustomed to do. Then recall to them the history of the resurrection of Lazarus, and afterwards that of Jesus Christ, and of his familiar appearances, during forty days, before so many persons. Finally, prove that it cannot be difficult to Him who has made man, to renew his existence. Do not forget the comparison of the grain of wheat

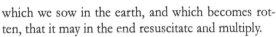

which we sow in the earth, and which becomes rotten, that it may in the end resuscitate and multiply.

It is not necessary to give these moral instructions to children to commit to memory, as we teach them their catechism; this method would tend to turn religion into an affected language, or at least into wearisome formalities; merely assist their minds, and put them in the way to find out these truths of themselves. They will be more their own, and more agreeable to them; they will impress themselves in a more lively manner. Profit by every occasion to develop to them what they yet see but indistinctly.

But take great care, for there is nothing more dangerous than to speak with contempt of this life, without letting them see, by every part of your conduct, that you speak seriously. In all ages, example has exercised an astonishing power over us; in infancy it is every thing. Children take great pleasure in imitating; they have not yet the habit which renders imitation difficult. Moreover, not being capable of judging of themselves of the depth of things, they judge much more of them from what they see in those who propose them to their observation, than by the reasons on which they are founded. Actions are even much more apparent than words; if then, they see things done which are contrary to what they are taught, they are accustomed to regard religion as a fine ceremony, and virtue as an impracticable idea.

Never take the liberty before children of making certain railleries on subjects connected with religion. We make game of the devotion of certain innocent persons: we are inclined to laugh at some things for which one consults his confessor, and at the penances imposed on him. You think that all this is innocent; but you deceive yourself; every thing leads to some consequence on this subject. We should never speak of God, nor of things which pertain to his worship, but with a seriousness and respect far removed from these liberties. We should never relax from a becoming decency, particularly on this subject. Often, those who are the most delicate in what relates to the world, are the most gross in what relates to religion.

When a child has reflected sufficiently to know himself, and to know God, connect together the historical facts with which he will already have been instructed, and from this mixture, he will find the whole of religion assembled in his head. He will remark with pleasure the connexion which exists between these reflections and the history of the human race; he will recollect that man is not made for himself; that his soul is the image of God; that his body has been formed with admirable nicety, by divine industry and power; soon he will recollect the history of the creation. Finally, he will believe that he is born with inclinations contrary to reason, that he is deceived by pleasure, carried away by anger, and that his body leads his soul contrary to reason, as an ungovernable horse carries his rider; whereas his soul ought to govern his body. He will perceive the cause of this disorder in the history of the sin of Adam; this history will make him expect the Saviour, who shall reconcile man with God: behold the foundation of religion.

To make children better understand the mysteries of the Christian religion, the actions, and the maxims of Jesus Christ, we must induce them to read the Gospel. We should then prepare them at an early age to read the word of God, to receive the body of Jesus Christ in the holy communion; we should propose to them as the principal foundation of their faith the authority of the church—the spouse of the Son of God, and the mother of all the faithful. It is this church, you will say to them, which we should hear, because the Holy Ghost enlightens her, in order that she may explain to us the Scriptures. We can only go to Jesus Christ when guided by her. Do not fail to read often to children, those parts of holy Scripture where Christ promises to uphold and to animate the church, that she may finally conduct her children into the ways of truth. Above all, inspire in girls that sober and temperate wisdom which St. Paul recommends to make them fear the snare of novelty, the love of which is so natural to their sex; prepossess them with a salutary horror for all singularity in matters of reli-

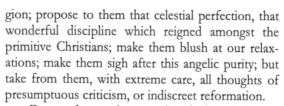

gion; propose to them that celestial perfection, that wonderful discipline which reigned amongst the primitive Christians; make them blush at our relaxations; make them sigh after this angelic purity; but take from them, with extreme care, all thoughts of presumptuous criticism, or indiscreet reformation.

Do not forget, then, to place before their eyes the Gospel, and the great examples of antiquity; but do not do it without having first proved their docility, and the simplicity of their faith. Return always to the church; show them with the promises which have been made to her, and with the authority which is given to her in the Gospel, how she has been preserved in all ages amidst so many attacks and revolutions; the inviolable succession of pastors and of doctrine, which manifest the accomplishment of the divine promises. Provided you can raise the foundation of humility, of submission, and of an aversion for all suspicious singularity, you will show with great advantage to young persons, all that is most perfect in the law of God, in the institution of the sacraments, and in the practice of the ancient church. I know that we cannot hope to give these instructions in all their extent, to all kinds of children; I only propose here to give them as exactly as we can according to the time, and the disposition of the minds that we have to instruct.

Superstition is to be feared for girls, but nothing

roots it out, or prevents it better than solid instruction. This instruction, however, ought to be confined within just bounds, and kept from all learned studies. It reaches much farther than is generally believed: a person may believe himself well instructed, who is not so, and whose ignorance is so great, that he does not even understand how deficient he is in the knowledge of Christianity. We must not suffer any thing to mix with our faith, or our practice of piety, which is not drawn from the Gospel, or authorised by the constant approbation of the church. We must discreetly fortify children against certain abuses, which are so common, that we are tempted to regard them as points of discipline presented by the church. We cannot entirely guard ourselves against them, if we mount not to their source, or do not know the institution of things, and the use which the saints have made of them.

Accustom girls, who are naturally too credulous, not to admit such histories as are without authority, and not to attach themselves to certain devotions, which an indiscreet zeal has introduced, without waiting for their being approved by the church.

The true means of teaching them how they ought to think on this subject, is not to criticise those things which a pious motive has often introduced, and which we ought for this reason to respect; but to show, without blaming them, that they have no solid

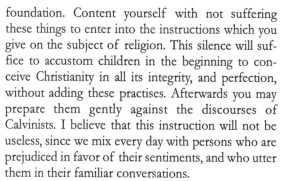

foundation. Content yourself with not suffering these things to enter into the instructions which you give on the subject of religion. This silence will suffice to accustom children in the beginning to conceive Christianity in all its integrity, and perfection, without adding these practises. Afterwards you may prepare them gently against the discourses of Calvinists. I believe that this instruction will not be useless, since we mix every day with persons who are prejudiced in favor of their sentiments, and who utter them in their familiar conversations.

They improperly impute to us, you will say to them, certain excesses as to images, invocation of saints, prayers for the dead, and indulgences. We are reduced to this by what the church teaches on baptism, confirmation, the sacrifice of the mass, penance, confession, the authority of priests, and on that of the pope, who is the first amongst them by the institution of Jesus Christ himself, and from whose see we cannot separate without quitting the church.

You see here all that is necessary to believe. What the Calvinists accuse us of adding, is not the Catholic doctrine. It is putting an obstacle to their re-union to wish to subject them to opinions which shock them, and which the church disavows; as if these opinions were a part of our faith. At the same time, never fail to show how the Calvinists have rashly condemned the most ancient and sacred ceremonies; add, that things newly instituted, being conformable to the ancient spirit, merit profound respect, since the authority which establishes them is always that of the immortal spouse of the Son of God.

In speaking thus of those who have drawn from the ancient pastors a part of their flock, under pretence of a reform, fail not to remark how much these proud men have forgotten human weakness, and how much they have rendered religion impracticable to all the ignorant, when they wish that every one should examine for himself, all the articles of the Christian doctrines in the Scriptures, without submitting to the interpretations of the church. Represent the holy Scriptures to the faithful, as the sovereign rule of their faith. We know as well as they do, you will say, "that the church must submit to the Scriptures;" but we say, "that the Holy Ghost aids the church in rightly explaining the Scriptures." It is not the church which we prefer to the Scriptures; but the explanation made of them by the whole church, to our own explanation. Is it not the height of pride and rashness in an individual, to fear that the church may be deceived in its decision, and not fear that he may himself be deceived in deciding against her?

Inspire children with the desire of knowing the reasons of the ceremonies, and of all the words which compose the divine office and administration of the sacraments. Show them the baptismal font; let them see the ceremony of baptizing. Show them, on holy Thursday, how we prepare the holy oil; and on holy Saturday, how we bless the water of the font. Give them a taste, not for sermons full of ornament, vain and affected, but for sensible and edifying discourses, as familiar sermons and homilies which make them clearly understand the letter of the Gospel; make them remark whatever is beautiful and touching in the simplicity of these instructions, and inspire them with a love of the parish church where the pastor speaks with benediction and with authority, however little he may have of talent or virtue. But at the same time, make them love and respect all the communities which concur in the service of the church. Never suffer them to mock at the habit, or at the state of the religious orders; show the sanctity of their institution, the utility which religion draws from them, and the prodigious number of Christians who, in these sacred retreats, tend to a perfection, which is almost impracticable in the engagements of the world. Accustom the imagination of children to hear death spoken of, to see a pall without fear, an open tomb, an expiring person, even those who are already dead, if you can do so without exposing them to sudden terror.

There is nothing more unhappy than to see many persons who have understandings and even piety, unable to behold death without trembling.

There are others who become pale at finding themselves making up the number thirteen at table, or of
having certain dreams, or at seeing the salt cellar
thrown down. The fear occasioned by all these imaginary presages, is a remnant of paganism. Show them
the vanity and folly of it: though women have not the
same occasions which men have to show their
courage, they ought nevertheless to possess it.
Cowardice is despicable at all times, for it has always
bad effects: a woman ought to be able to resist silly
alarms; she should be firm against certain unforeseen
dangers, and neither weep nor agitate herself but on
great occasions, and on these she must support herself by virtue. If we are Christians at all, surely it
teaches us not to be cowards. The soul of
Christianity, if we may use the expression, consists in
the contempt of this life, and the love of the other.

CHAPTER VIII.

INSTRUCTION ON THE DECALOGUE, ON THE SACRAMENTS, AND ON PRAYER.

HAT is most important, and ought unceasingly to be placed before the eyes of children, is Jesus Christ, the author and finisher of our faith, the centre of all religion, and our only hope. I do not mean here to say in what manner we ought to instruct them on the mystery of the incarnation; for this would lead me too far, and there are enough of books where we may find the foundation of all that is necessary to teach them. When the principles are formed, we must reform all the judgments and all the actions of the person whom we instruct, according to the model of Jesus Christ, who took a body like ours, to show us how to live, and how to die; showing us in his humanity what we ought to believe and practise. It is not necessary at every moment to compare the sentiments and actions of a child with the life of Jesus Christ. This comparison would become fatiguing and indiscreet: but we should accustom children to consider the life of Jesus Christ as our example, and his word as our law. Choose among his discourses and actions, those most adapted to children. If they are impatient at suffering any inconvenience, recall to their minds Jesus Christ on the cross. If they resolve not to undertake any disagreeable occupation, show them Jesus Christ working until the age of thirty years in a shop. If they wish to be praised and esteemed, speak to them of the opprobrium which was heaped upon our Saviour. If they cannot agree with those around them, represent Christ conversing with sinners and the most abominable hypocrites. If they testify any resentment, hasten to represent to them Jesus Christ dying on the cross, even for those who put him to death. If they suffer themselves to be carried away by an immodest joy, paint to them the sweetness and the modesty of Christ, whose whole life was so grave and serious. Finally, represent to them what Jesus Christ would think, and what he would say of our conversations, amusements, and most serious occupations, if he were still visible amongst us. What would be our astonishment, you will say, if he were to appear amongst us, when we are in perfect forgetfulness of his laws? But will not this happen to every one of us at our death, and to the entire world, when the hour of the universal judgment shall arrive? Then it will be well to paint to them the destruction of the whole universe — the sun obscured — the stars falling from their places — the consuming elements running in floods of fire, and the foundations of the earth shaken to the very centre. With what eyes then, you will add, ought we to regard this heaven which covers us — this earth which bears us — these edifices which we inhabit — and all these other objects which surround us, since they are reserved only for fire. Show them afterwards the tombs open, where the remains of the dead will be assembled; Jesus Christ descending on the clouds in high majesty; the book open, in which will be written the most secret thoughts of our hearts; that sentence pronounced in the face of all nations and of all ages; that glory which will open itself to crown eternally the just, and to make them reign with Jesus Christ upon the same throne. Finally, that lake of fire and brimstone, that night, and that eternal horror, that grinding of teeth, and that pain in common with the demons, which will be the everlasting portion of the wicked.

Do not fail fully to explain to them the decalogue; make them see that it is an abridgment of the law of God, and that they find in the Gospel what the commandments only contain by a more distant meaning. Tell them what counsel means, and prevent the children whom you instruct from flattering themselves, as men usually do, by a distinction which we

may push too far, between counsels and precepts.
Show them that counsels are given to make the precepts more easy, to strengthen man against his own
weakness, and to lead him from the edge of the
precipice, where he would be overbalanced by his
own weight; in short, that the counsels become
absolute precepts, for those who cannot on certain
occasions observe the precepts without the counsels.
For instance, those people who are too fond of the
pleasures of the world, and of idle associates, are
obliged to follow the evangelical counsels, to quit all,
and retire into solitude. Repeat frequently that "the
letter killeth, but the spirit giveth life;" that is to say,
the mere observance of outward forms is useless if
not animated by the spirit and love of religion.
Render this language clear and sensible—make them
understand that God is to be honored with the heart,
and not with the lips only; that ceremonies may be
regarded as the expression of the various acts of religion; that they nourish and excite devotion; but that
ceremonies are not religion itself; religion must be in
the mind: God seeks to be adored in spirit and in
truth; we must love him interiorly, and we must
behold in all nature, only God and ourselves. He
needs not our words or our postures, nor even our
money; that which he desires is ourselves; and we
should not only execute what the law ordains, but
execute it, so as to draw from it that fruit which it was

meant to produce by its promulgation. Thus, it is not
sufficient to hear mass, if we do not at the same time
understand that we are to unite with it the sacrifice of
Jesus Christ for us, and are not edified by every thing
which his immolation represents to us. Let us finish
by saying, that "all those who cry Lord, Lord, will not
enter into the kingdom of heaven;" but, if we do not
imbibe those true sentiments produced by the love of
God in our souls, such as renouncing temporal
goods, despising ourselves, and fearing the dangers of
the world, we make but a phantom of Christianity to
deceive ourselves and others.

Let us pass to the sacraments. I suppose you
have already explained all the ceremonies as they have
been performed in the presence of a child. This will
enable young persons to form some idea of the
object and utility of ceremonies. By this, you will succeed in making them understand the importance of
being a Christian, and how shameful and fatal it is to
us to act according to the spirit of the world. Recall
to their minds the promises of baptism, in order to
show them that the examples and maxims of the
world, so far from having any authority over us, ought
to render us suspicious of all that comes from a
source so much opposed to the maxims of the
Gospel. Do not fear to represent, like St. Paul, the
devil reigning in the world, and agitating the hearts of
men, by all those violent passions which make them

seek riches, glory, and pleasure. This pomp, you will
say to them, has still more of the devil in it than of
the world. This spectacle of vanity to which a
Christian ought never to open his heart, or even his
eyes, is in accordance with the spirit of the world.
The first step which baptism requires of us, is to
renounce all worldly pomp. Bring to recollection the
world, in spite of such solemn promises made to
God, fallen into a state of apostacy, like a religious, in
spite of his vows, who quits his cloister and habits of
penance, to enter again into the world. Tell them how
much we ought to trample under foot ill founded
contempt, impious raillery, and the violence of the
world; since confirmation rendered us soldiers of
Jesus Christ, to combat this enemy. You will continue:
the bishop has laid his hand upon you, to harden you
against the strokes of the most violent persecution.
He has administered a sacred unction to you, to represent the ancients, who anointed themselves with oil,
to render their members more supple and vigorous
when they went to battle; in short he has made the
sign of the cross on you, to show you that you ought
to be crucified with Jesus Christ. We are no longer,
you will say, in times of persecution, when those who
would not renounce the Gospel were put to death;
but the world, which cannot cease to be the world, no
more than it can cease to be corrupt, always indirect-
ly persecutes piety, holds out its snares, in order to

depress, insult and laugh at all piety, and thus render
its practise so difficult in all its degrees, that, in the
midst of a Christian nation, and even where it is
upheld by authority, we are in danger sometimes of
blushing at the name of Jesus Christ, and of swerv-
ing from the imitation of his life.

Represent strongly the happiness we possess in
being incorporated with Jesus Christ by the holy
eucharist. In baptism he makes us his brothers, in the
blessed eucharist he makes us his members; as he
gave himself in the mystery of the incarnation to the
human race in general, so he gives himself in the mystery of the eucharist, which so naturally follows the
incarnation, to each individual who is a faithful fol-
lower of him. All is true in the order of his mysteries;
Jesus Christ gives his flesh as truly as he has taken it;
but that which renders us unworthy of the body and
blood of our Lord is, to eat and to drink judgment to
ourselves, by eating the vivifying flesh of Christ without living by his spirit. "He, (said Christ,) who eateth
me, ought to live by me."

But what a misfortune, you will say, to stand in
need of the sacrament of penance; for one who has
been made the child of God should never commit
sin. Notwithstanding this celestial power which is
exercised on earth, and which God has given into the
hands of priests to retain, or to forgive sinners

according to their wants, being a great source of happiness springing from divine mercy, yet we ought to tremble for fear of abusing the gifts and patience of God. For we ought to desire ardently to nourish ourselves daily with the body of Jesus Christ, which is life, strength, and consolation to the just, but as for the remedy provided for souls in the state of sin, we should wish to arrive at so perfect a state of health as to diminish every day the want of it. The necessity, whatever we may be able to do, will be but too great; but it would be worse if we were every day to make a continual and scandalous circle from sins to penance, and from penance to sin. We cannot, then, question but that confession is instituted for our correction and improvement; otherwise, the words of absolution, however powerful they may be by the institution of Jesus Christ, would be by our indisposition only so fatal as to be our condemnation before God. A confession, without an interior change, very far from discharging the conscience from the load of its sins, on the contrary adds to those sins another, that of a monstrous sacrilege.

Make the children whom you educate, read the prayers for the dying, which are truly admirable; show them what the church does, and what she says, in giving Extreme Unction to the dying. What a consolation for them to receive again a renewal of the sacred unction for this last combat? But to render ourselves worthy of the graces of death, we must be faithful to the duties of life.

Admire the richness of the grace of Jesus Christ, who has not disdained always to apply the remedy to the source of the evil, in sanctifying the source of our birth, which is matrimony; that it was agreeable to our Lord to make a sacrament of this union of man and woman, which represents that of God with his creature, and of Jesus Christ with his church; that this benediction was necessary to moderate the brutal passions of men, to spread peace and consolation over all families, and to transmit religion as an inheritance from generation to generation.

Hence, we ought to conclude, that marriage is a very holy, and very pure state, though less perfect than virginity; that we ought to be called to it by Almighty God, and enter upon it not prompted by any desire of indulging carnal pleasures or worldly pomp; but with the laudable design of training up saints for heaven.

Let them hear you praise the infinite wisdom of the Son of God, who has established pastors to represent him on earth, to instruct us in his name, to administer to us the sacrament of his body and blood, to reconcile us again to him after our fall, and to form an uninterrupted succession of true and legitimate pastors, who still continue to conduct us in the right paths, that the church may be preserved in all ages. Show them what great reason we have to rejoice that God has given such great power to man. Tell them with what sentiments of religion they ought to respect the anointed of the Lord, the men of God, and the dispensers of his mysteries. If we should perceive in them, the least stain that can tarnish the lustre of their ministry, let us close our eyes and weep, let us even wish to wash away the stain with our blood. Their doctrine is not their own. Whosoever hears them hears Jesus Christ himself; and when they are assembled, in the name of Jesus Christ, to explain the Scriptures, it is the Holy Ghost who speaks by their mouth. Their time likewise is not their own. We should not therefore, wish to make them descend from their high ministry, in which they ought to devote themselves to the preaching of the word of God and to prayer, and act as mediators between God and man, in order to engage in worldly concerns. Much less is it permitted us to wish to derive profit from their revenues which are the patrimony of the poor, and the price of the sins of the people; but the most dreadful disorder is to wish to bring up their own relations or friends to this august ministry without any vocation or with a view to temporal interest.

It remains, to show the necessity of prayer; founded on our want of grace, which has been

already explained. God wills, we should say to the child, that we shall pray to him for grace, not because he is ignorant of our wants; but because he wishes to subject us to a demand, which excites us to acknowledge that want; it is thus an humiliation of our hearts, an acknowledgment of our misery and of our nothingness, it is that confidence in his goodness which he demands of us. This prayer, which he desires we should make, consists principally in the intention and desire; for he has no need of our words. We often recite many words without praying; and we often pray internally without pronouncing a single word. These words may nevertheless be very useful, for they excite in us thoughts and sentiments, if we are attentive to them. It is for this reason that Jesus Christ has given us a form of prayer. What a consolation to know from Jesus Christ himself, in what manner his Father wills that we should pray to him? Of what force must those demands be, which God himself puts into our mouth! Will he not grant that to us which he himself teaches us how to ask? After this, show how simple and how sublime this prayer is; how short, and full of all that we can expect from above.

The time for children to make their first confession, is a point that cannot be decided here! This will, in a great measure, depend on the state of their minds, but still more on the state of their consciences. As soon as they appear capable of instruction, they ought to be taught what is meant by confession; then wait for the first fault of any moment, that the child shall commit: when you should endeavor to excite in her soul the deepest sentiments of confusion and remorse. You will see that, being already instructed on confession, she will naturally seek to find consolation by confessing her fault to her confessor. Care must be taken by the confessor, to excite in her heart sentiments of repentance, and make her find in confession, a sensible consolation under her affliction, that this first confession may leave an extraordinary impression on her mind, and may prove a source of grace for all her future confessions.

First communion, on the contrary, it seems to me, ought to be made at the time when the child, having attained the use of reason, shall appear more docile, and more exempt from considerable faults. Here it is in these first fruits of faith, and of the love of God, that Jesus Christ makes himself the better felt, and that we taste through him the graces of communion. It ought to be a long time expected, that is to say, we ought to make the child hope for it from his earliest infancy, as the greatest good which he can have on earth, while he waits for the joys of heaven. I believe that it would be well to render the effect as solemn as possible, that we should appear to have our eyes fixed on the child during those days—that we

esteem him happy, that we take part in his joy, and that we expect from him a conduct above his age, for an action so great. But though it be necessary to prepare the child for communion, I believe that when he is prepared for it, we cannot too soon anticipate a grace so precious, before his innocence be exposed to dangers which will be prejudicial to him.

CHAPTER IX

REMARKS ON SEVERAL DEFECTS OF GIRLS.

E HAVE yet to speak of the care necessary to be taken in order to preserve girls from the defects common to their sex. They are generally brought up in indolence and timidity, which render them incapable of regular conduct. And first of all there is much affectation in the illfounded fears which habit afterwards confirms, as well as in the tears which they so readily shed. Contempt for these affectations may serve much to correct them, since vanity has so great a part in them.

It is also necessary to repress in them their tender friendships, little jealousies, excessive compliments, flatteries, anger, and officiousness. All these hurt them, and make them find every thing which is grave and serious, dry and austere. We should endeavor to make them study to speak in a short and concise manner. Good sense consists in retrenching all useless discourse, and in saying much in a few words;

instead of which, the generality of women say little in many words; they mistake a facility of speaking, and a vivacity of imagination, for wit; they do not choose between their thoughts; they put neither order nor connexion in them with regard to the things they have to explain; they are excited by almost all they say, and this passion makes them speak much. We can hope for nothing very good from a woman, if we do not reduce her to the habit of reflection, to examine her thoughts, to explain them in a short manner, and to know when to be silent.

Another cause which contributes much to the long discourses of women is, that they are generally cunning, and hence they use long discourses to gain their ends; they love duplicity; and why should they not love it, since they know no better prudence, and it is generally the first thing they are taught by example? They have naturally a pliability which makes them easily play off all kinds of dissimulation. Tears cost them nothing; their passions are lively, and their knowledge limited; hence, they neglect nothing to succeed, and the means which would not accord with minds well regulated, appear good to them. They seldom reason, in order to examine if a thing be desirable; but they are very industrious to obtain it.

Let us add, that they are timid, and full of false shame; this is another source of dissimulation. The means of preventing so great an evil, is never to put them in need of duplicity, and to accustom them ingenuously to express their inclinations on all proper subjects. Let them be free to make known their weariness when they feel it. Do not subject them to the necessity of pretending to like certain persons, or certain books, which do not please them.

It often happens that a mother, prejudiced in favor of her own spiritual director, is dissatisfied with her daughter until she goes under his direction; which the daughter adopts from a feeling of policy, though contrary to her taste. Above all things, a daughter should never be induced to believe that her parent wishes to give her a turn for the religious state; for this idea would remove all confidence due to parents, and would make the daughter believe that she was not beloved unless she complied with the wishes of her parents, and hence it would agitate her mind and compel her to act a forced and disguised character for many years. When they shall be so unhappy as to have acquired the habit of disguising their real sentiments, the best means of reforming the error is, to instruct them in solid maxims of true prudence; as we see from experience that to give a disgust for the frivolous fictions of romance, is to give a taste for useful and agreeable history. If you do not give them a rational curiosity, they will have a disorderly one; and according to the same reasoning, if you do not form their minds to true prudence, they will inevitably become

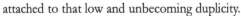

attached to that low and unbecoming duplicity.

Show them, by examples, how discreet they must be—how full of precaution; how firmly addicted to the legitimate means of succeeding, without however making use of the least shadow of deceit. Tell them that prudence principally consists in speaking little, in guarding more against ourselves than others; but not in making false representations or causing misunderstandings amongst persons. Upright conduct, and universal reputation for probity, attract more confidence and esteem, and consequently have in the end more advantages, even of a temporal nature, than the most skilful evasions we could possibly make use of. Nothing distinguishes a person so much or renders one so well fitted for the most arduous undertakings, as a sound and judicious probity and candor.

But you will add, that the object of this low and despicable deceit is either a mean quality which we should be ashamed to ask for, or a pernicious passion. When we wish only for what we ought to have, we desire it openly, and seek it by direct means, and with moderation. What can be more sweet, and more convenient, than to be sincere, always tranquil, at peace with ourselves, having nothing to fear, nothing to invent? Instead of which, a dissimulator is always in agitation, in a constant state of remorse, in danger; or in the deplorable necessity of covering one falsehood by a hundred others.

With all these shameful troubles, deceitful minds do not always escape the inconveniences which they fly from. Sooner or later they must pass for what they are. If the world be their dupe on any specific action, it is not so on the whole of their lives; they are always found out by some means or other. They are often duped by those whom they wish to deceive; for there are those who often appear to be blinded by others; and they believe themselves esteemed, when they are despised. But at least they cannot guard themselves against suspicion; and what can be more contrary to the advantages which wise self-love ought to seek, than to be always suspected? Enforce these things according to the occasion, by little and little, as they may be required, and according to the capacity of the mind to be instructed. You will observe, that deceitful cunning always proceeds from a mean heart and a little mind. They dissemble only because they wish to hide themselves, not being what they ought to be; or, wishing for legitimate things, they take unworthy means of obtaining them, for want of knowing how to choose honest means. Make children remark the impertinence of certain deceits which they see practised, and the contempt which they draw upon those who practise them: and finally, make them ashamed of themselves when you surprise them in any thing like dissimulation. From time to time, deprive them of what they wish for, because they sought to obtain

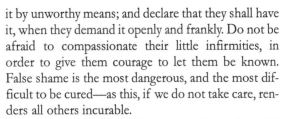

it by unworthy means; and declare that they shall have it, when they demand it openly and frankly. Do not be afraid to compassionate their little infirmities, in order to give them courage to let them be known. False shame is the most dangerous, and the most difficult to be cured—as this, if we do not take care, renders all others incurable.

Undeceive them, with regard to those shameful subtleties by which our neighbor is misled, whilst we escape the reproach of having deceived him. There is more meanness and trick in these refinements, than in the more common want of truth. Other persons practise, if I may use the expression, cunning with frankness; but these add to it a new disguise to authorize it. Tell a child that God is truth itself; that to tamper with the truth in words is to trifle with God; that we ought to render our words precise and exact; and speak little, that we may say only what is just, in order to show a due respect to the truth.

Guard yourself strictly from imitating those persons who applaud children when they display their wit by any deceitful cunning. Very far from finding these turns pretty, and from being diverted by them, you should reprove them severely, and be careful that their artifices shall not succeed, in order that they may be disgusted with them from their own experience. By the praise given for such faults, young minds are often persuaded that cunning is ability.

CHAPTER X

THE VANITY OF BEAUTY AND OF DRESS.

OTHING is so much to be feared in girls as vanity. They are born with a violent desire of pleasing. The paths which conduct men to authority and glory, being closed to them, they endeavor to compensate their loss by the agreeableness of their minds and persons. Hence their soft and insinuating conversation; hence it is that they aspire so much after beauty, and all the exterior graces, and are so fond of dress. A head-dress or a ribbon, a curl a little higher or lower, or the choice of a color, are to them matters of high importance.

These things are carried much farther in our nation (France) than in any other; the changeable humor which reigns amongst us causes a continual variety of fashions; thus they add to the love of dress, that of novelty, which has strange charms for their minds. These two follies uniting together, destroy all distinctions in society, and wholly derange the morals of the people. As soon as restraint is set aside in dress or in furniture, affectation only remains; and for the tables of individuals, it is what public authority can still less influence; each chooses according to his fortune, or rather without fortune, according to his ambition and his vanity.

This ambition is the ruin of families, which brings with it corruption of morals. On one side ambition excites in persons of low birth the passion of speedily acquiring a fortune, which they cannot do without sin, as the Holy Spirit assures us. On the other side, persons of quality finding themselves without resources, are guilty of horrible wickedness and meanness to support their expenses; by which they insensibly extinguish honor, faith, integrity, and good feeling, even between the nearest relations.

All these evils arise from the authority which vain women possess of deciding upon fashions. They look upon all those who wish to preserve the gravity and simplicity of the ancient manners, as Goths.

Study then, to make girls understand how the honor which is derived from good conduct, and from true capacity, is more estimable than that which is drawn from the dressing of the head or from the figure. Beauty, you will say, deceives the person who possesses it more than those who are dazzled by it; it troubles and intoxicates the soul. They more weakly idolize themselves, than the most impassioned lover does the person whom he loves. There is but a very small number of years between a beautiful woman, and one who is not so. Beauty can only be hurtful, if it serve not to procure for a girl an advantageous marriage. But, how will it serve her in this case, if it be not upheld by merit and virtue? She can only hope to marry a young fool, with whom she will be unhappy, at least, if her wisdom and her modesty do not make her seek amongst men, a mind well regulated and sensible as to solid qualities. Those persons who draw all their glory from their beauty, soon become ridiculous; they arrive without perceiving it, at a certain age, when their beauty fades—and they are charmed with themselves, though the world, far from being so, is disgusted with them. In short, it is as unreasonable to attach ourselves only to beauty, as it is to wish to rest all merit in our strength of body, as barbarians and savages do.

From beauty let us pass to dress. True grace does not depend on affected ornaments. It is true, that we should seek propriety, proportion, and decency in the dress necessary to cover our persons. But, after all, those garments which cover us, and which we may render convenient and agreeable, can never be ornaments which give true beauty.

I would even make young girls observe the noble simplicity which appears in statues, and in other figures which remain to us of the Greek and Roman women;

they would see there, how agreeable and majestic, the hair knotted up negligently from behind, and the long flowing draperies appear. It would even be well to let them hear painters, and others who have an excellent taste for antiquity, converse on these subjects.

If the mind had but raised itself ever so little above the prejudices of the world, it would soon learn to despise the idea of paying so much attention to the manner of decking the head-dress which is so unnatural. I well know that it is not to be expected nor desired that they should adopt the exterior of antiquity; it would be extravagant to wish for such a thing: but they may, without singularity, acquire a taste for this noble simplicity of dress so graceful, and also so agreeable to Christian manners. Thus, in conforming themselves exteriorly to present customs, they would know at least what they ought to think of those customs. They would conform to the world as a troublesome servitude, and would only give it what they could not refuse. Make them early and often remark the vanity and lightness of mind, which causes this inconstancy of fashion. It is no proof of a sound understanding, for example, to swell up the head with I know not how many heaps of millinery. True grace follows nature, and never restrains it.

But fashion destroys itself—it aims always at being perfect, and never finds itself so; at least, it can never stop when it is so. It would be reasonable if it only changed after having found a greater perfection, and a greater degree of taste in the commodity; but to change only for the sake of change, and without ceasing, is only to seek inconstancy and inconvenience, rather than true politeness and good taste. Generally speaking, fashions are governed wholly by caprice. Women have the decision of them. They only are to be believed regarding them. Thus minds the most frivolous and least instructed, lead others. They neither choose nor abandon a thing by rule. It is sufficient for a thing to be a long while in fashion, to be so no longer; and that another, how ridiculous soever it may be, having a title to novelty, should take its place, and be admired. After having displayed this foundation, demonstrate the rules of Christian modesty. We learn, you will say, from the sacred writings, that man was born in the corruption of sin: his body laboring under a contagious malady, is an inexhaustible source of temptation to the soul. Jesus Christ teaches us to place all our virtue in the fear and denial of ourselves. We might say to a girl, would you hazard your soul, and that of your neighbor, for a silly vanity? Have a horror, then, for an uncovered neck, and for all other immodest actions. Though we should even commit these faults without any bad design, it is at least a vanity; it is an immoderate desire of pleasing. We can neither justify our vanity before God, nor before man, for conduct so bold, so scandalous, and so contagious

to others. Does this blind desire of pleasing become a
Christian soul, which ought to regard as idolatry every
thing which would turn it from the love of its Creator,
and the contempt of creatures? But, when we seek to
please, what do we pretend? Is it not to excite the passions of men? Have we it always in our power to stop
them, if they go too far? Ought we not always to
impute to ourselves the consequences; and do not
they always go too far if they be ever so little
inflamed? You prepare a mortal and a subtle poison;
you infuse it into all the spectators, and you believe
yourself innocent. Add the example of persons
whose modesty has rendered them commendable, and
of those whose want of it has been prejudicial to
them. But above all, permit nothing in the exterior of
girls which is above their condition. Strictly repress all
their fancies. Show them to what danger they expose
themselves, and how they are despised by wise persons, when they thus forget what they are.

What remains to be done, is to undeceive girls
respecting their wit. If we do not well guard against
it, when they have vivacity, they will intrigue, they will
speak on every thing; they will decide on those works
which are least proportioned to their capacities; they
will affect to be tired by delicacy. A girl ought never to
speak but from real occasion, and with an air of
doubt and diffidence. She ought not to speak of
things which are above the common knowledge of

girls, although she may be instructed in them. However good her memory may be, however great her vivacity, her pleasant turns, and her facility of speaking gracefully, will be common with a great number of other women of little discretion, and who may be very despicable. But let her conduct be exact and orderly, with a well regulated mind. Let her know how to be silent, and how to conduct herself. This quality, which is so rare, will distinguish her amongst her sex. For delicacy and affectation of disgusts, must be repressed, by showing that good taste consists in accommodating ourselves to whatever is useful.

Nothing is estimable but good sense and virtue. One and the other regard disgust and weariness, not as a laudable delicacy, but as the weakness of a sick mind.

Since we must live with unpolished minds, and in occupations which are not delightful, reason, which is the only real delicacy, consists in rendering ourselves homely with those who are so. A mind which tastes politeness, but which knows how to render itself above it, when it is necessary to apply to things more solid, is infinitely superior to those delicate minds which are overpowered by their disgusts.

CHAPTER XI

INSTRUCTION TO WOMEN ON THEIR DUTIES.

E ARE now come to the detail of those things on which a woman ought to be instructed. What are her employments? She is charged with the education of her children: of sons, until they come to a certain age; of the daughters, until they marry or enter into religion; of the conduct of the domestics, of their manners, of their service, of the detail of expense, of the means of doing every thing with honor and economy; sometimes to manage estates and receive rents.

The science of women, like that of men, ought to be limited to that instruction which relates to their duties. The difference of their employments ought to make that of their studies. We should then limit the instruction of women to the things which we have just spoken of. But a woman desirous of knowledge, will feel that this is giving very limited bounds to her curiosity; she deceives herself in this, and it is because she knows not the importance and the extent of those duties in which I propose to instruct her. What discernment is it not necessary to possess, in order to enter into the nature and the dispositions of each of her children; to find the most proper manner of conducting herself with them, in order to understand their humor, their inclination and their talents; to guard against their growing passions, to induce them to good habits, and to cure their errors? What prudence ought not she to have, to acquire and preserve an authority over them, without losing their friendship and confidence? And is it not also necessary that she should be fully acquainted with those persons whom she has about them? Undoubtedly the mother of a family ought to be fully instructed in religion; and she should have a mind matured, firm, regulated, and experienced in government.

Can we doubt, that women are charged with all these cares, since they fall naturally on them during the life even of their husbands who are occupied abroad? They regard them still more nearly, if they become widows. In short, St. Paul attaches their salvation to the education of their children, so much so that he declares it to be by them that they will be saved.

I do not here explain all that women ought to know for the education of their children, because this memorial of it is sufficient to make them feel how extensive is the knowledge which they ought to have.

To this government let us join economy. The greater number of women neglect this, as a mean employment, suitable only to the wife of a peasant or a farmer, or to a housekeeper. Women who are nourished in delicacy, abundance, and idleness, are indolent, and disdain all these details: they imagine there is no difference between a country life, and that of the savages of Canada. If you speak to them of the sale of wheat, or the culture of the earth, or the different sources of revenue, the levying of rents, and the other duties of a landlord; of the best manner of managing farms, or of establishing stewardships, they fancy you wish to reduce them to occupations altogether unbecoming their station.

It is nevertheless from ignorance, that we despise the science of economy. The ancient Greeks and Romans, who were so intelligent, generally speaking, and so polished, instructed themselves in this with great care. The greatest minds amongst them have composed, from their own experience, books which we now possess, in which they have given all the details of agriculture. We know that their conquerors disdained not to labor, and to return to the plough when they retired from the triumph. This is so far different from our customs, that we should scarcely know how to believe it, if we could find in history any pretext for doubting it. But is it not natural that we

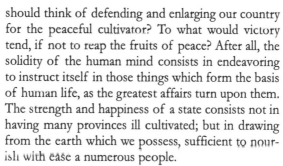

should think of defending and enlarging our country for the peaceful cultivator? To what would victory tend, if not to reap the fruits of peace? After all, the solidity of the human mind consists in endeavoring to instruct itself in those things which form the basis of human life, as the greatest affairs turn upon them. The strength and happiness of a state consists not in having many provinces ill cultivated; but in drawing from the earth which we possess, sufficient to nourish with ease a numerous people.

It is undoubtedly necessary to possess a more powerful and cultivated genius, in order to instruct ourselves thoroughly in all the arts which relate to economy, and to be in a state to govern a whole family, which is, as it were, a little republic, than to reason about fashions, and to exercise ourselves in the little arts of conversation. That is a sort of mind that is very despicable, which can go no farther than to speak well. We see every where women whose conversation is full of solid maxims; but who, for want of having applied themselves to employment early in life, are full of nothing but frivolity in their conduct.

But we must guard against the opposite fault. Women run the risk of being extreme in every thing. It is well to accustom them from their infancy to have charge of something, to keep accounts, to see the manner in which we purchase, and to know how every thing is made, in order to be of use; but let us

take care that economy does not degenerate into avarice. Show them particularly, all the ridicule which this passion draws upon itself. Tell them, that avarice gains but little, and that it is very dishonorable; that a reasonable mind ought to seek only, in a frugal and laborious life, to avoid the shame and the injustice attached to a prodigal and ruinous conduct. We should retrench superfluous expenses, only to be in a state to be more liberal in those things which convenience, or friendship, or charity inspire. It is often a great gain to know when to lose properly. It is good order, and not certain sordid savings, which make great profits. Do not fail to represent the great error of those women, who unwillingly spare themselves a taper, whilst they suffer themselves to be deceived by their house-keeper in the general expenditure of their affairs. Say as much on neatness as on economy; accustom girls to suffer nothing about them which is unclean or disorderly. Make them remark the least disorder in the house; make them even observe that nothing contributes more to economy and propriety, than to keep every thing in its place. This rule appears trifling, nevertheless it would profit a great deal if it were well attended to. What you have need of, you lose no time in seeking; in this there is neither trouble, nor dispute, nor embarrassment—you put your hand upon it immediately; and when you have done with it, you replace it where you had found it.

This good order makes one of the principal points in neatness. Nothing strikes the eye more than to see every thing in its proper place. On the other hand, the place we give to every thing is that which best suits it, not only on account of its agreeableness to the eye; but still more for its preservation. It is less used, and is less subject to be spoiled by accident; it is even properly preserved. For example, a vase will not be dusty, or in danger of being broken, when it is put in its place immediately after it is used. The same spirit of exactness, which makes us arrange every thing in its place, also makes us neat. Add to these advantages, that of its being a means of keeping servants in better order. Moreover, it is a great object to render their service prompt and easy, and so take from yourself the temptation of being impatient on account of the delay which arises from things being deranged and not to be found. But at the same time, be careful to avoid all excess of elegance and arrangement.

Arrangement, when it is moderate, is a virtue; but when we devote our time too much to it, then it becomes trifling and shows a want of mind. Good taste rejects excessive delicacy. It treats small things as small, and is not wounded by them. You will laugh, then, in presence of children, at those trifles of which some women are so fond; and which insensibly cause them such extravagant expenses. Accustom them to simplicity and propriety, which are easy to practise. Show them the best manner of doing every thing; but show them still more how to overlook things. Tell them what lowness and littleness of mind it shows, to scold when a dish happens to be ill seasoned, or a curtain ill folded, or a chair too high or too low.

It undoubtedly shows a better turn of mind to be voluntarily unpolished, than to be over delicate on things of no importance. This ill-founded delicacy, if we do not repress it in women of mind, is yet more dangerous with regard to their conversation, than in all the rest. The generality of people are insipid and wearisome to them. The least defect of politeness appears to them dreadful. They are always sneering and disgusted. We should make them early understand, that there is nothing so injudicious as to judge superficially of a person by his manners, instead of examining his mind, sentiments, and useful qualities. Make them see, by repeated experience, how much a country farmer with clumsy appearance, or even with his ridiculous ill-timed compliments, if he have a good heart, and a well regulated mind, is more estimable than the most polished courtier, who under a refined politeness, conceals an ungrateful, unjust heart—capable of all kinds of dissimulation and baseness. Add to this that there is always a weakness in those minds which are continually fatigued and disgusted. There are not many persons whose conversation is so bad, that we cannot draw something good from it. Though we ought to choose better when we are free to choose, we have yet sufficient consolation, when we are reduced to seek it, by making such people speak of what they know; and persons of intellect can always draw instruction from those even who are the least enlightened. But let us return to those things in which it is necessary to instruct girls.

CHAPTER XII.

CONTINUATION OF THE DUTIES OF WOMEN.

HERE is an art in making yourself obeyed, which is of great consequence. You must know how to choose your domestics from among those who possess both honor and religion. You must know the functions to which you wish to apply them; the time and trouble necessary to be given to every thing; the manner of doing it well; and the expense necessary for it. You would do wrong to scold a servant, because what you had desired was not accomplished in less time than it was possible to do it in; or if you do not know, in some degree, the price and quantity of the articles which are required, you are in danger of being the dupe or the plague of your domestics. You must therefore have some knowledge of their occupations.

It is also necessary to know their dispositions, in order to be able to govern their minds, and to guide all this little republic, which is generally very tumultuous, in a Christian-like manner. There must also be sufficient authority; for the more unreasonable people are, the more necessary it becomes to hold them in subjection under the influence of fear. But as they are Christians, and even your brothers in Jesus Christ, and consequently as you ought to respect them as his members, you are obliged to use authority only when persuasion fails.

Endeavor then, to make your people love you, without low familiarity. Enter not into conversation with them; but do not be afraid of speaking to them on their wants with affection, and without pride. Let them feel assured of always finding counsel and compassion from you. Do not reprimand their defects too harshly, never appear much surprised or cast down by their defects, but on the contrary, show them that you hope they will be cured of them. Make them gently understand your reasons, and bear patiently with them in their service, that you may be able to convince them coolly and without impatience, and that you speak to them less on account of your own convenience, than for their interest. It will not be easy to accustom young persons of quality to this mild and charitable conduct: for impatience and the ardor of youth, joined to a false idea given to them of their birth, make them look upon their domestics as objects worth little less than their horses. They do not

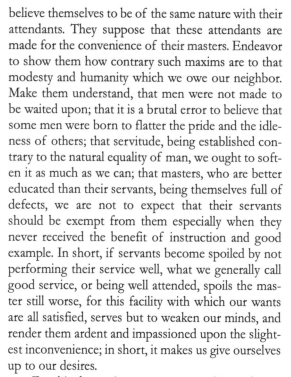

believe themselves to be of the same nature with their attendants. They suppose that these attendants are made for the convenience of their masters. Endeavor to show them how contrary such maxims are to that modesty and humanity which we owe our neighbor. Make them understand, that men were not made to be waited upon; that it is a brutal error to believe that some men were born to flatter the pride and the idleness of others; that servitude, being established contrary to the natural equality of man, we ought to soften it as much as we can; that masters, who are better educated than their servants, being themselves full of defects, we are not to expect that their servants should be exempt from them especially when they never received the benefit of instruction and good example. In short, if servants become spoiled by not performing their service well, what we generally call good service, or being well attended, spoils the master still worse, for this facility with which our wants are all satisfied, serves but to weaken our minds, and render them ardent and impassioned upon the slightest inconvenience; in short, it makes us give ourselves up to our desires.

For this domestic government, nothing is better than to accustom girls to it at an early age. Give them something to manage, on condition that they render you an account of it. This confidence will please them exceedingly; for young persons receive incredible pleasures when we begin to confide in them, and to make them enter into some real business. We see a fine example of this in the reign of Queen Margaret. This princess recounts in her memoirs, that the most lively pleasure she experienced in her life, was to perceive that the queen, her mother, began to converse with her when she was yet young, as if she had been a grown person. She felt herself transported with joy, at being taken into the confidence of the queen, and of her brother, the duke of Anjou, regarding the secrets of the state. She had known until then, only the plays of children. Suffer a girl even to commit some faults in these affairs, and be willing to sacrifice something for her instruction; make her gently remark what she should have done or said, to avoid the inconveniences into which she had fallen; relate to her your past experience, and be not afraid to tell her of the faults, similar to her own, which you made in your youth. By this means you will inspire her with confidence, without which education must be a constrained formality.

Teach a girl to read and write correctly. It is shameful, but very common, to see women, who have intellect and politeness, not know how to pronounce well what they read. They either hesitate, or they sing out when reading; instead of which, they ought to pronounce in a simple and natural tone, but firm and united. They fail still more grossly in orthography, or in the manner of forming or connecting their letters in writing. At least accustom them to make their lines straight, and to form their characters clear and legible. It is also necessary that a girl should understand the grammar of her own language. It is not necessary that she should learn it by rule, as scholars learn Latin in class. Accustom them only, without affectation, not to take one tense for another; to make use of proper terms to explain their thoughts with order and clearness, and in a short and concise manner. You will by this means enable them, one day or other, to teach their children to speak well without any study. We know that in ancient Rome, the mother of the Gracchi contributed much, by a good education, to form the eloquence of her children, by which they became great men.

They ought also to know the four first rules of arithmetic. They would become useful to yourself, by often making them keep your accounts. It is an occupation for which many persons have no taste whatever, but the habit, acquired in infancy, joined to the facility of doing quickly by the help of rules, all sorts of accounts, even the most difficult, will diminish this distaste. We well know, that exactness in accounts often makes the good order of a house.

It would be well, also, that they should know something of the principal rules of justice. For example, the difference there is between a legacy and a donation; they should know the nature of a contract; a substitution; a division of co-heirs; the principal rules of the rights and customs of the country in which they live, to render those acts valid; that which is meant by individual, and that which is meant by common property; what is meant by goods movable, and immovable. If they marry, all their principal affairs will turn on this.

But at the same time, show them how incapable they are of going deeply into the difficulties of rights; show them how the right itself, from the weakness of the mind of man, is full of obscurity and of doubtful rules; how jurisprudence varies; how all that depends on judges, however clear it may appear, becomes uncertain; how the best terminated suits are frequently ruinous and insupportable. Show them the agitation of the courts of justice, the madness of chicanery, the pernicious turns and subtleties of the proceedings, the immense expenses they incur, the misery of those who plead, the industry of the advocates and solicitors, to enrich themselves by impoverishing the parties. Add to this, that an affair, good in itself, becomes bad by reason of the means employed in it. The opposition of the maxims of justice between one tribunal and another. If you are sent back to the grand chamber, your process is gained; if you go to the court of requests, it is lost. Do not forget the conflicts of the jurisdiction, and the danger we are in of

applying many years to the council, to know where
we are to plead. Finally remark the difference of
opinion between advocates and judges on the same
cause; in the consultation you will have gained the
cause, but your trial condemns you to pay the costs.

All this seems to me very important, as it may be
a means of preventing women from feeling too much
impassioned on these affairs, and from giving themselves up blindly to certain advisers, enemies of
peace, when they are widows, or mistresses of their
fortune, in any other state. They ought to listen to
people who understand their business, but not to be
wholly guided by them.

It is right that they should mistrust themselves in
the process which they are persuaded to undertake.
Let them consult persons of a more enlarged knowledge, who are more attentive to the advantages of an
accommodation; and finally, let them be persuaded
that the principal point in a law suit, is to foresee the
inconveniences, and to know how to avoid them.

Girls of birth, who have considerable fortunes,
ought to be instructed in the duties of the landholders of their estates. Tell them every thing that can be
done to prevent abuse, violence, chicanery, and
deceit, so common in the country. Join to this knowledge, the means of establishing little schools, and
charitable meetings for the relief of the sick and the
poor. Show them also the traffic which we may some-

times establish in certain countries, to diminish misery; but above all, how we may procure for the people solid instruction, and good government. All this would demand details too long to be given here.

In explaining the duties of landholders, do not forget their rights; tell them what is meant by a fief, a lord of the manor, a vassal, homage, rent, rights of field rent, lots and sales, indemnity, passing away estates and acknowledgments, plans of estates, and other things of the like nature. This knowledge is necessary, since the government of estates consists entirely on these things.

After this instruction, which ought to hold the first place, I believe that it is not useless to suffer girls, according to their leisure and the extent of their capacity, to read profane history; it is even a means of giving them a disgust for comedies and romances. Give them, then, the Grecian and Roman histories; they will there see prodigies of courage and disinterestedness; do not let them be ignorant of the history of France, which has its beauties; mix those of the neighboring countries, and the relations of distant countries which are judiciously written.* All this serves to enlarge the mind, and to raise the soul to grand sentiments, provided we avoid vanity and affectation.

*It is scarcely necessary to say, that the author would have added the history of her own country, of whatever nation she might be, had he adverted to his work being translated. *Translator.*

It is generally thought, that a girl of quality, who is well brought up, should learn Italian and Spanish; but I see nothing less useful than this study, unless she be attached to the person of some Spanish or Italian princess, like our queens of Austria and of Medicis; otherwise, these two languages serve for little but to enable them to read dangerous works, calculated to augment their defects. There is much more to be lost than to be gained by this study. That of Latin would be much more rational, for it is the language of the church; some fruit would arise from it, and an inestimable consolation from understanding the sense of the words of the divine office at which they so often assist.

Those even who seek for beauty in language would find it much more perfect and more solid in Latin, than in the Italian or Spanish, where there remains a frivolity of mind, and a vivacity of imagination without rule. But I would only have those girls learn Latin, who have a firm judgment and modest conduct; who would know how to study it for what it is worth; renounce vain curiosity, and hide what they would have learned, and who would seek it only for their edification.

I would permit them also, but with great choice, the reading of works of eloquence and poetry, if I saw that they had a taste for it, and that their judgment was sufficiently solid to keep them to the true use of these things. But I should fear to embroil their lively imaginations too much by them, and I would have an exact sobriety reign throughout; every thing which makes love felt, the more it is softened and enveloped the more it appears dangerous.

Music and painting require the same caution. All these arts arise from the same genius and the same taste. For music, we know that the ancients believed nothing to be more pernicious to a well regulated republic, than to suffer an effeminate melody to be introduced; it enervates men; it renders the soul soft and voluptuous; its languishing and passionate tones give so much pleasure, as to cause the soul to abandon itself wholly to the attraction of the senses. It was for this reason, that the Spartan magistrates broke all the instruments, whose harmony was too delicious; and this was one of their most important regulations; it was on this account that Plato sternly rejected all the delicious tones which entered into the music of the Asiatics. How much stronger reason is there, that Christians ought never seek its pleasure? They ought to have a horror of such impassioned diversions.

Poetry and music, if we take from them all that does not tend to a right end, might be employed very usefully to excite in the soul sublime and lively sentiments of virtue. How many poetical works have we, which the Hebrews sung? The canticles were the first monuments which preserved to us any tradition of divine things before the Scriptures. We have seen how powerful music has been amongst the Pagans, to raise the soul above vulgar sentiments. The church has believed that it could do nothing better to console her children, than by singing the praises of God. We cannot then give up these arts which even the Spirit of God has consecrated. Sacred music and poetry would be the best of all means to give a disgust of profane pleasures; but from the false prejudices of our nation, a taste for these arts would not be without danger. We must then hasten to make a young girl feel that we see very plainly, from such impressions, how many charms we find in music, without going out of pious subjects. If she have a voice, and a genius for the beauty of music, we cannot hope to keep her always ignorant of it. The prohibition would only increase the desire for it. It is better to give a regulated course to the torrent, than to undertake to stop it. Painting, amongst us, turns more easily to good; it also has a privilege for women; without it, their works could not be well conducted. I know that they might be reduced to such simple works as would not require this art; but in the design which it seems to me we ought to have, to occupy the mind, at the same time that we employ the hands, of women of quality, I should wish that every pleasure were seasoned by some work of industry and of art. These works cannot produce beauty, if the knowledge of painting does not conduct them. Hence it is, that almost all that we now see in stuffs, laces, and embroidery, are in bad taste: all is confusion, without design or proportion. These things pass for pretty, because they cost much labor to those who make them, and much money to those who buy them; their splendor dazzles those who see them from a distance, or who do not understand them. Women have made the rules which govern the fashions; those who should contest them would only pass for visionaries. They would, nevertheless, unde ceive themselves, if they were to consult the painters, and by this means put themselves in a state of receiving greater pleasure at a moderate expense, by making works of noble variety and beauty, which would be above the irregular caprice of fashion.

They ought equally to fear and despise idleness. Let them remember that the primitive Christians, of every condition in life, worked, not to amuse themselves, but for occupation, following serious and useful employments. Natural order, the penance imposed on the first man, and from him on all his posterity; that of which the new man, who is Jesus Christ, has left us so great an example; every thing engages us to a laborious life, each according to his condition.

We ought to consider, in the education of a girl, her condition, the situation in which she will probably pass her life, and the profession which she may be likely to embrace. Let us be careful that she conceive no hopes above her condition. There are not a few persons whom it has cost dear to have raised their hopes too high; that which would otherwise have rendered them happy, becomes disgusting from the moment they have conceived the hope of a state above them. If a girl be destined to live in the country, turn her mind early to the occupations which engage her there, and suffer her not to taste the diversions of the city; show her the advantages of a simple and active life; if she be of a moderate condition in the city, do not let her mix with those of the court; this commerce would only serve to make her acquire an unbecoming and ridiculous air. Keep her within the bounds of her condition, and give her for a model those who best succeed in it; form her mind to those things which will occupy her during her life; teach her the economy of the house, the care which it is necessary to take of the receipts of rents for town and country, what regards the education of children, and, in short, the detail of other occupations in affairs of commerce, in which you foresee that she may have to enter, when she will be married. If, on the contrary, she should express an inclination for a religious life, of her own free choice, turn all her education to the state to which she aspires. Put the powers of her mind and body to serious trials before you allow her to enter her novitiate, which is a kind of engagement with respect to the honor of the world. Habituate her to silence; exercise her obedience in things contrary to her humor or inclination; try by degrees to see what are her qualifications for the state she has in view; accustom her to a coarse, serious, and laborious life; show her how free and happy persons in religion are, who can dispense with a great deal of that vanity and attention which, in the world, is in some degree indispensable. In one word, accustom her to poverty; but make her feel the happiness that Jesus Christ has revealed for the poor in spirit. Be careful not to leave a taste for any vanity of the world when she shall quit it. Without exposing her to trials that are dangerous in themselves, discover to her the thorns concealed under the false pleasures which the world gives, and show her how many persons are there unhappy in the midst of pleasures.

CHAPTER XIII

ON GOVERNESSES.

 FORESEE that this plan of education will be thought by many people to be a chimerical project. It would be necessary, they will say, to possess discernment, patience, and extraordinary talents to execute it. Where are the governesses capable of understanding it? And where are they who can follow it? But I beg them to consider attentively, that when we undertake a work on the best education to be given to children, we are not to give imperfect rules. It is not then to be objected, that we aim at what is most perfect in this research.

It is true, that every one cannot reach the practise so far as our thoughts go, when we put them on paper. But, in fine, though even we cannot arrive at perfection in this work of education, it is not useless to know what perfection is, and to endeavor to obtain it. It is the best means of approaching towards it. On the other hand, this work does not suppose an

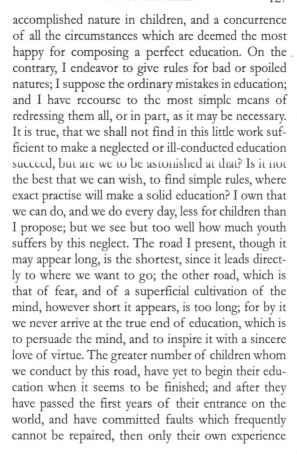

accomplished nature in children, and a concurrence
of all the circumstances which are deemed the most
happy for composing a perfect education. On the
contrary, I endeavor to give rules for bad or spoiled
natures; I suppose the ordinary mistakes in education;
and I have recourse to the most simple means of
redressing them all, or in part, as it may be necessary.
It is true, that we shall not find in this little work sufficient to make a neglected or ill-conducted education
succeed, but are we to be astonished at that? Is it not
the best that we can wish, to find simple rules, where
exact practise will make a solid education? I own that
we can do, and we do every day, less for children than
I propose; but we see but too well how much youth
suffers by this neglect. The road I present, though it
may appear long, is the shortest, since it leads direct-
ly to where we want to go; the other road, which is
that of fear, and of a superficial cultivation of the
mind, however short it appears, is too long; for by it
we never arrive at the true end of education, which is
to persuade the mind, and to inspire it with a sincere
love of virtue. The greater number of children whom
we conduct by this road, have yet to begin their education when it seems to be finished; and after they
have passed the first years of their entrance on the
world, and have committed faults which frequently
cannot be repaired, then only their own experience

and reflections lead them to the maxims with which this restrained and superficial education had not been able to inspire them. We ought to observe that this first trouble, which I require to be taken for children, and which persons without experience consider as overpowering and impracticable, spares consequences much more vexatious, and smooths obstacles which become insurmountable, in consequence of an education less exact and uncultivated. In fine, let us consider, that to execute this project of education, the question is less to do things which require great talents, than to avoid gross faults which we have remarked in detail. It is an important point not to press children to be assiduous about them, to observe them, to inspire them with confidence, to answer clearly and with good sense their little questions, to leave them to act naturally, that we may the better know them, and inform them with patience, when they deceive themselves, or commit some fault. It would be unreasonable to expect that a good education should be conducted by a bad governess; it is undoubtedly enough to give rules which will enable a moderate subject to succeed. It is not demanding too much of this subject to desire that she should have at least good sense, a rational humor, and a true fear of God; such a governess will find nothing in this writing subtle and abstracted. Though she should not even understand the whole of it, she will conceive it generally, and that will be sufficient. Make her read it many times; take the trouble to read it with her; give her the liberty of stopping you, whenever she does not understand you, and when she is not persuaded of its truth; afterwards put her to practise it, and as she loses sight, in speaking to the children, of the rules in this work which she had agreed to follow, remark to her gently upon it in private. This application will at first be painful to you; but if you are the father or mother of the child, it is your essential duty. On the other hand, you will not for a long time have any great difficulty in it; for this governess, if she be sensible, and well disposed, will learn more in a month by her practise and your advice, than by long reasonings; she will soon walk in the right road. You will have also this advantage as a release to you, that she will find in this little work the principal discourses which it will be necessary to hold with the children on the most important maxims, all ready, so that she will only have to follow them. Thus she will have before her eyes a collection of conversations which she ought to have with the children, on those things which are most difficult to make them understand. It is a kind of practical education, which will conduct her by the hand. You may also make use of the HISTORICAL CATECHISM, of which we have already spoken. Only make the governess whom you form, read it several times; and above all, endeavor to make her understand the preface well, that she may in the end enter into this method of teaching. It must, however, be owned, that these persons of moderate talent, to whom I confine myself, are rare to find. But we must have a proper instrument of education; for the most simple things are not to be learned of themselves; and they turn always to what is wrong in an ill formed mind. Choose, then, from your own family, or from your tenants, or from your friends, or from a well regulated seminary, some girl whom you believe capable of being trained; think of forming her at an early age for this employment; and keep her some time about you, that you may prove her, before you confide to her a trust so precious. Five or six governesses, trained in this manner, would soon be capable of forming a great number of others. We should find ourselves, perhaps, deceived in some of these persons; but finally, in the great number, we should always find sufficient to make amends for this disappointment, and we should not be in the extreme embarrassment in which we now perpetually find ourselves. Religious and secular communities, whose institutions have been founded for the education of youth, might also enter upon this system which is so well calculated to form their mistresses of boarders, and mistresses of schools.

But although the difficulty of finding governesses be great, it must be owned that there is another greater, the irregularity of the parents. Every thing is useless, if they themselves will not concur in this work. The whole foundation is, that they give to their children right maxims and edifying examples. This is what we can only hope for in a small number of families. We see in the greater number of houses only confusion, and changes; a number of domestics, amongst whom reigns as much contradiction of mind, as between their superiors. What a frightful school for children! Often a mother, who passes her life at cards, in going to the theatre, and in improper conversations, complains, in a grave tone that she cannot find a governess capable of educating her daughters. But what can the best education do for girls when they see before their eyes such a mother? And again, we often see parents who, as St. Augustine says, themselves lead their children to public spectacles and other diversions, which cannot fail to disgust them with a life of seriousness and occupation, in which even these parents wish to engage them. They thus mix poison with salutary food. They speak of wisdom; but accustom the lively imaginations of their children to the violent emotions caused by the impassioned representation of music, after which, they are unable to apply themselves. They give them food to excite the passions, and then they are surprised when innocent pleasures become insipid. After this, they still expect their children's education to succeed; and they look upon it as an unnecessary austerity, if this mixture of good and evil be not permitted. Is it not imputing a false honor to ourselves, to desire a good education for our children, without choosing to take the trouble of it; or to subject ourselves to the rules necessary for it?

Let us finish by the portrait which the wise man has given of a virtuous woman:

PROVERBS XXXI. *Who shall find a valiant woman? The price of her is as of things brought afar off, and from the uttermost coasts. The heart of her husband trusteth in her, and he shall have no need of spoils. She will render him good and not evil, all the days of her life. She hath sought wool and flax, and hath wrought by the counsel of her hands. She is like the merchant's ship, she bringeth her bread from afar. And she hath risen in the night, and given a prey to her household and victuals to her maidens. She hath considered a field, and bought it: with the fruit of her hands she hath planted a vineyard. She hath girded her loins with strength, and hath strengthened her arm. She hath tasted and seen that her traffic is good: her lamp shall not be put out in the night. She hath put her hand to strong things, and her fingers have taken hold of the spindle. She hath opened her hand to the needy, and stretched out her hands to the poor. She shall not fear for her house in the cold of snow: for all her domestics are clothed with double garments. She hath made for herself clothing of tapestry; fine linen and purple is her covering. Her husband is honorable in the gates, when he sitteth among the senators of the land. She made fine linen and sold it, and delivered a girdle to the Chananite* (or merchant). *Strength and beauty are her clothing, and she shall laugh in the latter day. She hath opened her mouth to wisdom, and the law of clemency is upon her tongue. She hath looked well to the paths of her house, and hath not eaten the bread of indolence. Her children rose up and called her blessed: her husband, and he praised her. Many daughters have accumulated riches: thou hast surpassed them all. Favor is deceitful and beauty is vain: the woman that feareth the Lord, she shall be praised. Give her of the fruit of her hands; and let her works praise her in the gates.*

However the extreme difference of manners, the brevity and coldness of figures, render this language at first rather obscure, we find in it a style so lively and so full, that we soon become charmed with it, if we examine it more minutely; but what I wish most to be remarked, on the authority of Solomon, the wisest of all men, is, that the Holy Spirit himself, whose words are so magnificent, makes us admire, in a rich and noble woman, the simplicity of her manners, her economy, and labor.

FENELON'S EPISTLE

TO A

LADY OF DISTINCTION,

ON THE

EDUCATION OF HER DAUGHTER.

MADAM:

A S you desire, I will endeavor to give you my ideas upon the education of your daughter.

Had you many to educate, the task would be embarrassing, as your connexions in life oblige you to absent yourself more from your family than you would wish. In that case, you should choose some convent where the education of boarders is studiously attended to. But as you have an only daughter to educate, and as God has rendered you perfectly adequate to the undertaking, I think she may receive from you a better education than in any convent. The eyes of a wise, tender and Christian mother, undoubtedly discover blemishes that would escape others. As these qualities are very rare, the most prudent step a mother can take, is to confide her children's education to some regular community. Frequently, mothers have not learning requisite to educate their daughters, or if they have, they do not strengthen it by the example of a serious and Christian conduct, without which the most solid instructions make no impression. With you the reverse is the case, you think but of serving God; religion is the first of your cares, and you will only inspire your daughter with what she will see you practise. Hence I must except you from the general rule, and prefer you, for her education, to any convent. There is even a great advantage in her receiving her education from you. The most subtle of poisons is vanity; and even in a convent, if the greatest precaution be not taken, this vice, so dangerous for young persons, may have its charms. She would hear the scholars speaking of the world as of a scene of enchantment; and nothing can leave a more pernicious impression on the mind than this deceitful image. It is held up at a distance, as the centre of pleasure and enjoyment, whilst its disappointments are carefully concealed. The world never dazzles so much as when viewed at a distance, before it has been really seen, and without being forewarned of its seduction. Hence, I would fear a worldly convent more than the world itself. On the contrary, if a community have preserved the fervor and regularity of its institute, a young girl may be brought up in it in profound ignorance of the world. It would, undoubtedly, be a happy ignorance were it to last for ever; but if this girl, on leaving the convent, is to return to the paternal mansion, in which the spirit of the world abounds, nothing is more to be feared than this sudden surprise. A girl who has been disengaged from the world by being ignorant of it, and in whose heart virtue has not had time to strike deep roots, will soon be tempted to believe that the charms of a worldly life have been studiously concealed from her. She leaves the convent like a person who has been brought forth from a dark dungeon where he has been pent up all his life, and exposed to open day. Nothing can be more dazzling than this sudden transit from one extreme to another. Far better is it for a girl to be introduced by degrees to the manners of the world, under the protection of a discreet and virtuous mother who will only suffer her to see what is proper for her—who will point out as occasion shall offer the dangers of the world, and who will teach her by her own example, to use it with moderation, and as necessity requires. I esteem the education given in good convents; but I have a decided preference to that given by a learned and virtuous mother, if she have it in her power to give the necessary attendance. I conclude, therefore, that your daughter is better situated near you, than she can possibly be in the very best convent. But there are very few mothers to whom I would venture to give the same advice.

I allow that this education would be attended with many dangers, unless you take care in the choice of persons you suffer to be about your daughter. Your domestic occupations, and the duties of civility abroad, will not permit you to have your child always under your eyes. You cannot always take her with you; but I recommend you, to quit her as little as possible. If you entrust her to light, indiscreet, or disorderly women, they will teach her more evil in eight days, than you will be able to teach her good in several years. These persons, who, for the most part, have only received a very moderate education themselves, will educate your child in the same defective manner. They will speak in her presence with too great freedom, and your daughter will not fail to notice every thing that is said or done, and will endeavor to do the same. They will lay down the most false and dangerous maxims. The child will hear slander, lying, suspicious and wrangling words; she will see jealousies, animosities, incompatibility of temper, and sometimes false and dangerous devotions without any correction of the grossest faults. These persons, moreover, are of a mean and servile spirit: they will not fail to please the child by base and dangerous flattery. I confess, that the education given in the most indifferent convents, would be superior to this domestic education; but I am supposing that you will never lose sight of your daughter, except in cases of absolute

necessity, and that you will have a person on whom
you can depend to take the responsibility in your
absence. This person must have sufficient sense and
virtue to know how to maintain a certain degree of
authority sufficient to keep others that may be
employed in their strict duty; to correct the child
when necessary, without incurring her displeasure,
and to acquaint you, at your return, of whatever is
deserving your notice. I allow, that such a person is
not easy to be found; but you must attend to this
point, and do not refuse the necessary expense to
make her situation as agreeable as possible. I know
that you may, on many occasions, be disappointed;
but you must rest satisfied with the essential qualifications, and tolerate such defects as may be mixed
with these accomplishments. Without the assistance
of a person of this description, believe me, you will
never succeed in the education of your daughter.

As your daughter shows great quickness of
parts, great facility, penetration and candor, I fear she
may acquire a taste for ambition, and an excess of
vain and dangerous curiosity. You will permit me to
make one reflection, which ought not to wound your
delicacy of feeling, as it does not regard you. Women,
in general are more passionately fond of the ornaments of the mind than of those of the body. Those
who are capable of study, and who have hopes of dis-
tinguishing themselves, are more anxious about their

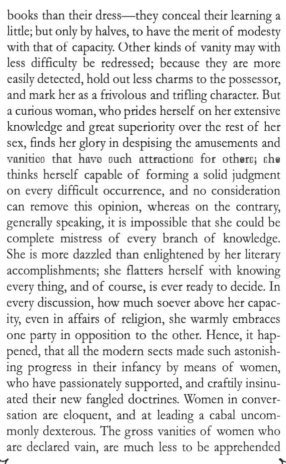

books than their dress—they conceal their learning a
little; but only by halves, to have the merit of modesty
with that of capacity. Other kinds of vanity may with
less difficulty be redressed; because they are more
easily detected, hold out less charms to the possessor,
and mark her as a frivolous and trifling character. But
a curious woman, who prides herself on her extensive
knowledge and great superiority over the rest of her
sex, finds her glory in despising the amusements and
vanities that have such attractions for others; she
thinks herself capable of forming a solid judgment
on every difficult occurrence, and no consideration
can remove this opinion, whereas on the contrary,
generally speaking, it is impossible that she could be
complete mistress of every branch of knowledge.
She is more dazzled than enlightened by her literary
accomplishments; she flatters herself with knowing
every thing, and of course, is ever ready to decide. In
every discussion, how much soever above her capacity, even in affairs of religion, she warmly embraces
one party in opposition to the other. Hence, it happened, that all the modern sects made such astonishing progress in their infancy by means of women,
who have passionately supported, and craftily insinu-
ated their new fangled doctrines. Women in conversation are eloquent, and at leading a cabal uncom-
monly dexterous. The gross vanities of women who
are declared vain, are much less to be apprehended

than those serious and refined vanities which effect a
display of ready wit and superior abilities, which
appear brilliant with a certain show of solid merit. It
will therefore be necessary, incessantly to recall your
daughter to a judicious simplicity. It will be enough
for her to possess that knowledge of her religion
which is sufficient firmly to believe it, and punctually
to follow it in practice, without any pretensions to
dispute on such subjects. She must only hear the
church, and follow faithfully those who preach her
doctrine. Her confessor should be a man edifying by
the regularity of his manners and skilled in the science of conducting souls to God. She must shun the
conversation of indiscreet women who take upon
themselves to argue points of doctrine; and she
should be taught how unbecoming and dangerous
this liberty is. She should hold in utter abhorrence all
pernicious publications, without wishing even to
examine why they are condemned. She should learn
to be diffident of herself, and to fear the snare of
curiosity and presumption. She should be earnest in
her supplications to God, that she may become poor
in spirit, frequently recollected, and at all times sub-
missive. She should take pleasure in being corrected
by her wise and discreet friends, even in her most
decided judgments, and should possess the talent of
listening with deference to others. I would much
sooner have her learned in the manner of keeping the

accounts of the house, than in the school disputes of
theologians on the subject of grace. Let her be occupied with needle work, with tapestry that may be useful in the house, and may habituate her to live happi-
ly at home, without too much communication with
this dangerous world; but do not permit her to argue
on divinity to the great risk of her faith. All will be
lost if she set herself up for a wit, or if she become
disgusted with domestic employments. The valiant
woman, says the wise man, spins, finds happiness in
her own family,—is silent, believes and obeys; she disputes not against the church.

I am perfectly satisfied, that you will be able, as
occasions shall present themselves, to introduce certain well-timed reflections on the impropriety and
indecency observable in the affected display of erudi-
tion in a certain class of females. These observations
you must make purposely to preserve your daughter
from foundering against the same dangerous rock.
But as the authority of a mother must be carefully
preserved, and as the wisest lessons do not always
carry conviction to a daughter, when contrary to her
inclinations, it would be advisable to engage ladies of
approved merit in the world, and your true friends, to
speak with you in the presence of your daughter on
this subject, without appearing to allude to her in the
most distant manner. You must concur in blaming the
vain and ridiculous character of women who affect to

pass for learned, and who betray a marked partiality
for innovators in religion. These indirect instructions
will, in all appearance, leave a more lasting impression
on her mind, than all the discourses you could direct
to her personally.

With regard to dress, I would wish you might be
able to instil into your daughter's mind a true taste for
moderation. There are some characters, so decided
among women, and so extravagant, that mediocrity to
them is of all things the least supportable. They
would prefer an austere and marked simplicity, which
would show a spirit of reform and censure of the
world, in renouncing the extravagance of the reigning
fashion, sooner than walk in the just medium, which
they look upon as an evident want of taste, and as a
stupid and insignificant line of conduct. It is,
notwithstanding, true, that the point most enviable,
and at the same time the most rare, is to aim at that
wise and just mediocrity, which will equally avoid
both extremes, which will give to the world what it
can reasonably expect, without trespassing the limits
which moderation has prescribed. True wisdom, with
regard to furniture, equipage, and dress, is to avoid
singularity by avoiding all extremes. Dress yourself,
you may say to your daughter, so as not to pass in the
eyes of the world as a slovenly person without taste;
but at the same time, let no affectation of dress, nor
pomp appear in your exterior: thus you will show that

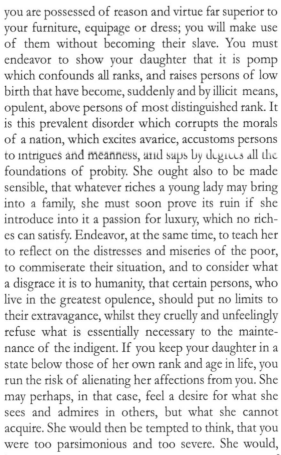

you are possessed of reason and virtue far superior to
your furniture, equipage or dress; you will make use
of them without becoming their slave. You must
endeavor to show your daughter that it is pomp
which confounds all ranks, and raises persons of low
birth that have become, suddenly and by illicit means,
opulent, above persons of most distinguished rank. It
is this prevalent disorder which corrupts the morals
of a nation, which excites avarice, accustoms persons
to intrigues and meanness, and saps by degrees all the
foundations of probity. She ought also to be made
sensible, that whatever riches a young lady may bring
into a family, she must soon prove its ruin if she
introduce into it a passion for luxury, which no riches can satisfy. Endeavor, at the same time, to teach her
to reflect on the distresses and miseries of the poor,
to commiserate their situation, and to consider what
a disgrace it is to humanity, that certain persons, who
live in the greatest opulence, should put no limits to
their extravagance, whilst they cruelly and unfeelingly
refuse what is essentially necessary to the mainte-
nance of the indigent. If you keep your daughter in a
state below those of her own rank and age in life, you
run the risk of alienating her affections from you. She
may perhaps, in that case, feel a desire for what she
sees and admires in others, but what she cannot
acquire. She would then be tempted to think, that you
were too parsimonious and too severe. She would,

then, perhaps, be impatient to see herself at her own disposal, that she might have her fling in the vanity of the world. You would succeed far better by keeping her in a just medium, and this line of conduct must meet with the approbation of all prudent and sensible persons. She will then see that you wish her to have every thing that becomes her; that you deny nothing through sordid economy; that you have a just consideration for her, and that your only wish is to preserve her from imitating the extravagance of certain persons, whose vanity knows no bounds.

It is extremely essential that you do not yield to any immodest fashions which are unworthy of Christianity. You may call in arguments from good breeding, and from interest, to support in this case the cause of religion. A young lady, who forms a connexion with a vain, irregular, and light character, may be said to make a sacrifice of all future happiness and content. Hence, she ought to make herself as agreeable as possible to persons of an opposite cast. But to find a steady, wise, and discreet companion for life, she must be extremely correct and modest, and suffer nothing light or foolish to transpire in her comportment. For where is the man, who has any pretensions to wisdom and prudence himself, who can admire a young woman, who, to judge from appearances, is full of vanity and conceit, and whose virtue is at best rather equivocal?

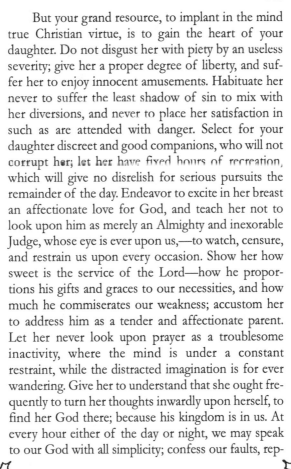

But your grand resource, to implant in the mind true Christian virtue, is to gain the heart of your daughter. Do not disgust her with piety by an useless severity; give her a proper degree of liberty, and suffer her to enjoy innocent amusements. Habituate her never to suffer the least shadow of sin to mix with her diversions, and never to place her satisfaction in such as are attended with danger. Select for your daughter discreet and good companions, who will not corrupt her; let her have fixed hours of recreation, which will give no disrelish for serious pursuits the remainder of the day. Endeavor to excite in her breast an affectionate love for God, and teach her not to look upon him as merely an Almighty and inexorable Judge, whose eye is ever upon us,—to watch, censure, and restrain us upon every occasion. Show her how sweet is the service of the Lord—how he proportions his gifts and graces to our necessities, and how much he commiserates our weakness; accustom her to address him as a tender and affectionate parent. Let her never look upon prayer as a troublesome inactivity, where the mind is under a constant restraint, while the distracted imagination is for ever wandering. Give her to understand that she ought frequently to turn her thoughts inwardly upon herself, to find her God there; because his kingdom is in us. At every hour either of the day or night, we may speak to our God with all simplicity; confess our faults, represent our necessities, and take the necessary measures for their speedy amendment. We ought to listen to God in the interior silence of the soul, saying: *I will listen to the Lord within myself*. We must endeavor to acquire the happy and excellent habit of walking always in his presence, and of doing all things, great or small, for his love; and as often as we perceive that we have lost sight of his presence, so often must we renew it. We must peaceably endeavor to remove the thoughts that distract us as soon as ever we remark them, without distracting our minds still more with violent efforts, or with too great uneasiness on account of their frequent and importunate returns. We must be patient with ourselves, and not feel disheartened at our levity and inconstancy. Involuntary distractions do not remove us from God; no disposition is more agreeable to him than the humble patience of a soul ever ready to recommence her good resolutions to return to him. Your daughter will soon enter into a true spirit of prayer, provided you will facilitate the practise by opening to her the door. No sallies of wit, no great effort of the imagination, no exquisite and sentimental affections are necessary, which God gives and takes away as he sees expedient. When we know no other sort of prayer but that which consists in sensible and pleasing affections, so well calculated to flatter our interior, we soon become discouraged; for this sort of prayer is very soon exhausted, and then we seem to think that all is lost. But tell her, that prayer resembles a simple, familiar, and affectionate intercourse of society; or to speak more properly, that it is this society itself.

Habituate her betimes to unbosom herself before her God, to make use of every method to converse with him, to entertain him, to address him with confidence, as she would speak freely and without reserve to a person she loves, and who as sincerely loves her. The far greater part of persons who limit themselves to a certain form of prayer as before God as they are before persons they respect, and whom they only see occasionally through formality, without either loving them, or being loved by them; the whole visit passes in ceremonies and compliments; both parties are uneasy, tired and impatient to be set at liberty. Whereas persons truly interior are, with God, as with the most intimate friends; they do not measure their words, because they know to whom they are speaking; every thing proceeds from the simplicity and abundance of the heart. We speak to him of the most interesting subjects of his own glory and of our salvation. We mention to him the faults we wish to correct, the duties we wish to fulfil, the temptations we wish to overcome, and the artifices of our own self love, we wish to repress. In a word, we tell him every thing, and he hears every thing; we pass in review his commandments, and even his counsels, to

see how we have observed them. This is no longer a ceremonial intercourse, but a free conversation of true friendship. Then God becomes the friend of the heart; a parent, in whose breast a child finds consolation, a spouse with whom, through grace, one and the same spirit is found to animate them. There we humble, without discouraging ourselves; we unite a sincere confidence in God, with a total diffidence of ourselves; there we never forget the correction of our faults; but we forget to listen to the deceitful counsels of self love. If you instil and nourish this simple and solid piety into your daughter, she cannot fail of making most rapid progress. I remain, &c.

THE PORTRAIT

OF A

VIRTUOUS AND ACCOMPLISHED WOMAN,

PAINTED BY THE INIMITABLE FENELON

IN HIS XXII. BOOK OF "TELEMACHUS,"

IN THE CHARACTER OF ANTIOPE,

AND FORMED ON THE SYSTEM OF EDUCATION LAID

DOWN IN THE PRESENT WORK, MUST PROVE HIGHLY ACCEPTABLE.

A woman loveliest of the lovely kind,
In body perfect, and complete in mind.

 NTIOPE is mild, simple and wise; her hands despise not labor; she forsees things at a distance; she provides against all contingencies; she knows when it is proper to be silent; she acts regularly and without hurry; she is continually employed, but never embarrassed, because she does every thing in its proper season. The good order of her father's house is her glory, it adds a greater lustre to her than beauty. Though the care of all lies upon her, and she is charged with the burden of reproving, refusing, retrenching (things which make almost all women hated,) yet she has acquired the love of all the household; and this, because they do not find in her either passion, or conceitedness, or levity, or humors as in other women. By a single glance of her eye, they know her meaning, and are afraid to displease her.

The orders she gives are precise; she commands nothing but what can be performed; she reproves with kindness, and in reproving encourages. Her father's heart reposes upon her as a traveller, fainting beneath the sun's sultry ray, reposes himself upon the tender grass under a shady tree.

Antiope is a treasure worth seeking in the most remote corners of the earth. Neither her person nor her mind is set off with vain ornaments; and her imagination, though lively, is retained by her discretion. She never speaks but through necessity; and when she opens her mouth, soft persuasion and simple graces flow from her lips. When she speaks, every one is silent; and she is heard with such attention, that she blushes, and is almost inclined to suppress what she intended to say; so that she is rarely ever heard to speak at any length.

FENELON'S PLAN OF EDUCATION
REDUCED TO PRINCIPLES.

I. Study well the *constitution* and *genius* of your child.

II. Follow *nature*, and proceed easily and patiently.

III. Suffer servants, as little as possible, to be with her, much less to terrify her with frightful stories.

IV. Give her a *pleasing* idea of virtue, and a *frightful* picture of vice.

V. Let her *diet* be plain and wholesome, and her exercise and meals justly regulated.

VI. Watch the first appearances of *reason*, and carefully cultivate them.

VII. Labor sweetly to correct her childish *passions* and *prejudices.*

VIII. Use no *dissembling* arts to pacify or persuade her.

IX. Recommend an *open, sincere character*, and show an abhorrence for *duplicity.*

X. If she be *witty*, do not flatter her; if *dull*, do not discourage her.

XI. Endeavor to rectify her *judgment*, fortify her reason, and restrain her *imagination.*

XII. To all her *questions* give short and opposite answers.

XIII. Promote useful *curiosity*; but suppress every sentiment of *vanity* and *self-conceit.*

XIV. Instil into her first principles of *politeness, modesty*, and every *Christian virtue.*

XV. Show the deformity and baseness of a *lie*, and how detestable is the character of a *liar.*

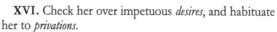

XVI. Check her over impetuous *desires*, and habituate her to *privations*.

XVII. Teach her to do all things in *order*, and with *method*; but nothing in a *hurry*.

XVIII. Insinuate the principles of *economy*; but impose a hatred of *parsimony*.

XIX. Improve the feelings of her *heart*, by conducting her to objects in distress.

XX. Let her see that *personal* charms are not to be compared with *mental* accomplishments.

XXI. Her *dress* and *studies* should both be regulated according to her rank in life.

XXII. *Civility* is due to all; *familiarity* only to a few.

XXIII. The *less* she esteems herself, the *more* she will be admired by others.

XXIV. Teach her to *copy* in herself, what she most admires in her companions, and carefully to avoid what may be offensive in them.

XXV. A habit of industry and occupation will secure her from many temptations.

XXVI. Make her *virtuous* in youth, and she will be a support to her parents in their old age.

XXVII. Let *virtue* and *religion* have the first place in her heart.

XXVIII. Let her *early years* be devoted to solid piety.

XXIX. Instruct her of how much greater *value* is her *inmortal soul* than this *perishable world*.

XXX. And that sooner than risk the *former*, she must sacrifice the *latter*.